The Early Spread of Christianity in Central Asia and the Far East

Analecta Gorgiana

640

Series Editor
George Anton Kiraz

Analecta Gorgiana is a collection of long essays and short monographs which are consistently cited by modern scholars but previously difficult to find because of their original appearance in obscure publications. Carefully selected by a team of scholars based on their relevance to modern scholarship, these essays can now be fully utilized by scholars and proudly owned by libraries.

The Early Spread of Christianity in Central Asia and the Far East

A New Document

Alphonse Mingana

gorgias press
2010

Gorgias Press LLC, 954 River Road, Piscataway, NJ, 08854, USA

www.gorgiaspress.com

Originally published in

2010 ၀

ISBN 978-1-61719-589-1 **ISSN 1935-6854**

Extract from (1925)

Printed in the United States of America

THE EARLY SPREAD OF CHRISTIANITY IN CENTRAL ASIA AND THE FAR EAST: A NEW DOCUMENT.

BY A. MINGANA, D.D.

ASSISTANT KEEPER OF MANUSCRIPTS IN THE JOHN RYLANDS LIBRARY, AND SPECIAL LECTURER IN ARABIC IN THE UNIVERSITY OF MANCHESTER.

Foreword.

I.

BEFORE venturing into the subject of the evangelisation of the peoples of Mongolian race, it would be useful to examine the ethnological state of the powerful agglomeration of clans inhabiting the adjacent lands lying on the eastern and western banks of the river Oxus. There we meet with constant struggles for supremacy between two apparently different races, distinguished by the generic appellations of Irān and Tūrān. They were somewhat loosely separated by the historic river, the shallow waters of which in a summer month, or in a rainless season, proved always powerless to prevent the perpetual clash of arms between the warring tribes of the two rivals whose historic habitat lay on its eastern and western borders. In Arabic and modern Persian literature, the literature of those Persians who, after the Arab invasion, made of Arabic their literary vehicle, we are given to understand that this feud between two neighbouring peoples dates from pre-historic times. According to the Persian national epic, the *Shāhnāmah* of Firdausi, this struggle for supremacy goes back to Feridūn, the Noah of the Iranian race, who distributed the earth to his three sons—Salm, Tūr, and Īraj,—corresponding roughly with Shem, Ham, and Japhet, of the Hebrew Bible. By a cowardly stratagem the first two named elder brothers made away with

Īraj, to whom the land of Irān was allotted by his father. Feridūn, seeing the lifeless body of Īraj, his youngest son, swears vengeance on his two other children.

During Sasanian and even Parthian times, the period which falls within the compass of our present study, we still find the bitter struggle going on between the two sworn rivals, with alternate defeats and victories. The unifying religious bond of Islam brought for a time to the two rivals that peace and concord which neither community of interests, nor exhausting wars, were able to accomplish. This was the state of affairs till the advent of the Turanian Seljuḳs, and the Tartar Mongols, who inflicted a crushing defeat upon their hereditary enemies, the Iranians, and put an end to the old feud. In the time immediately preceding and following the onrush of the peoples beyond the Oxus, a good section of the Iranians had enjoyed a somewhat precarious independence under the more or less important dynasties of the Ṭāhirids, Ghaznawids, Ṣaffārids, and Sāmānids.

The introduction of Christianity among the above peoples goes back to a very early period, and so far as the Persian section of them is concerned, to the post-Apostolic times. We are now in a position to speak of the subject in a much more confident way than our predecessors did even twenty-five years ago, thanks to new and important publications which were unknown to them. We will here refer only to two works of outstanding importance—the *Synodicon Orientale*, and the History of Mshīḥa-Zkha, edited and translated, the first by J. B. Chabot,[1] and the second by the present writer.[2] The first work gives us as signatories of an Eastern Council held in A.D. 424, the names of the Bishops of four large towns in the immediate proximity of the Oxus,—Ray, Naishābur, Herat, and Merw ;—and the second reveals to us the fact that in A.D. 225 there were more than twenty Bishoprics in North Mesopotamia and in Persia, one of which among the Dailams near the Caspian Sea. The date 225 is referred to in connection with the epoch making year in which the first Sasanian

[1] *Notices et Extraits des Manuscrits*, 1902.

[2] *Sources Syriaques*, 1908, i. 1-168. Sachau gave, in 1915, a German translation of it in *Abhandlungen d. Preus. Akad. d. Wiss.* where he rechristened the work under the name of *Chronik von Arbela.* This Chronicle and the Synodicon are the main sources of his other study entitled "Zur Ausbreitung des Christentums in Asien, 1919, in No. 1 of the same "Abhandlungen."

king gained a decisive victory over Artaban, the last monarch of the Parthian dynasty.[1] From the third century down to the time of Chingis Khan, the activity of the East-Syrian and Persian converts to Christianity slowly but surely worked to diminish the immense influence of the priests of the hundred and one primitive cults of Central Asia, the most important of whom were the mobeds of Zoroastrianism and the wizards of Shamanism.

That the men interested in the missionary work which brought Western civilisation and beliefs to the farthest end of the Far East were mainly animated by religious enthusiasm we have no reason to doubt, and St. Jerome sums up the feelings of the early Christian missionaries of those regions by saying of their converts "*Hunni discunt Psalterium, Scythiae frigora fervent calore fidei.*"[2] Similar would be the religious devotion of those Christian communities about which Bardaisan[3] and Eusebius of Cæsarea[4] wrote as existing in Bactria, Parthia, and Gilān, on the Caspian Sea. But alongside of these warm followers of Jesus of Nazareth, there might have been also Christian men who travelled from Mesopotamia and Persia, in pursuit of commercial undertakings and earthly gain. It seems, however, that there were hardly among them any of those Phœnician Syrians, of whom St. Jerome wrote, "*Negotiatoribus et avidissimis mortalium Syris,*"[5] or "*Usque hodie autem permanet in Syris ingenitus negotiationis ardor, qui per totum mundum lucri cupiditate discurrunt.*"[6] Whatever means were employed by those early pioneers of Christianity, there is no reason for denying the important fact that in an amazingly short space of time, they introduced their religious convictions literally into the remotest confines of ancient Asia.

The nerve-centre of this movement towards Christian beliefs in Central Asia and even in India was undoubtedly the province of Adiabene situated East of the Tigris, beween two of its historic tributaries: the Greater and the Lesser Zabs. The Capital of this province was Arbel the numerous Jewish population of which was so

[1] *Sources Syriaques*, pp. 106-107 of my edition.
[2] Epist. cvii. *Patr. Lat.* xxii. 870.
[3] *Book of the Laws* (in *Pat. Syr.*), ii. 606-609.
[4] *Prepar. Evang.*, vi. 10, 46.
[5] Ep. cxxx. 7, *Patr. Lat.* xxii. 1112.
[6] In Ezech. viii. xxviii. 16, *Patr. Lat.* xxv. 255.

much in the ascendant at the beginning of the Christian era that for some time it forced on this part of the old Assyrian Empire a reigning dynasty of Jewish blood.[1] Even as far West as the right banks of the Tigris, near the more modern town of Mosul, the Jews had erected a fortress called *ḥisna 'ebrāya* "The Hebrew Fort,"[2] which existed down to the Arab invasion.

Christianity had penetrated into Arbel immediately after the Apostolic age, because the ordination of its first Bishop, Pḳīdha, goes back to the end of the first century.[3] The city played for the countries extending East, North, and South of the Tigris a role no less important (if somewhat less known) than that played by Edessa in the trans-Euphratic provinces of the Roman and Persian Empires in particular, and in Syria and Palestine in general. Sozomen[4] asserts that the majority of the inhabitants of Adiabene were Christians: *Haec Persidis regio est, maxima ex parte* (ὡς ἐπίπαν) *a Christianis habitata.*

It is not sufficiently realised by modern scholars that the immense majority of the members of the Nestorian Church living east of the Tigris were of Persian, and not Semitic or Aramean birth and extraction. Many were born of Christian parents who originally belonged to the Zoroastrian faith, and many others were only themselves converts from Zoroastrianism. Some of these converts retained their Iranian names, but some others changed them on the day of their baptism into Christian appellations formed by means of one or two compounds underlying elements of Christian beliefs. The Middle Persian or Pahlawi was in constant use among Persian Christian Doctors. In 420 Ma'na, a student of the School of Edessa, translated Syriac works into Pahlawi.[5] About 470 another Ma'na of the same school wrote in Pahlawi religious discourses, canticles, and hymns, to be sung and recited in Churches.[6] Even the ecclesiastical Canons of the Nestorian Church were sometimes written in Persian and translated

[1] Josephus, *Antiq. Jud.* l. xx., c. iv.

[2] Mshīḥa-Zkha, *ibid.* i. p. 87 of my edition; *Narsai Homiliae*, vol. ii., pp. 408-410 of my edition; *Chron. Minora* in *C.S.C.O.* p. 24; and *Book of Chastity*, 32, 13 (edit. Chabot).

[3] Mshīḥa-Zkha, *ibid.* p. 77.

[4] *Eccl. Hist.* in *Pat. Graec.*, lxvii., 965.

[5] *Chronique de Seert* in *Pat. Orient.* v. 328-329.

[6] *Ibid.* vii. 117.

into Syriac by some later author; so the Canons of Simon, Metropolitan of Riwardashir, who died about 670, were originally composed by him in Pahlawi, and were afterwards translated into Syriac by a monk from Beith Ḳatrāye.[1]

In the following pages we propose to lay before our readers a comprehensive list of all the Syriac and Christian Arabic passages that we have been able to collect on the subject of the evangelisation of the Turks, and other peoples of Turanian stock. It is hoped that they will serve as a kind of introduction to the present document, which deals with the same theme. By a curious irony of fate the word "Turk" has come to be synonymous with "Muslim" in almost all the Dictionaries of modern European languages. In reality many forefathers even of the Ottoman Turks of Constantinople and Anatolia were zealous Christians before Muḥammad was born. The documents of the Christian literature with which we will exclusively deal we divide into three distinct parts: (1) Historians; (2) Synods and Bishoprics; (3) Surviving traces and Monuments.

1. Historians.

(*a*)

The oldest document in Syriac literature relating to Christianity in Central Asia is the memorable sentence of Bardaiṣān uttered not much later than A.D. 196 concerning the Christians of Gilan, South-West of the Caspian Sea, and those of Bactria, the ancient name of the country between the range of Hindu Kush and the Oxus:

"Nor do our (Christian) sisters among the Gilanians and Bactrians have any intercourse with strangers."[2]

This proves decisively that towards the end of the second century the Edessene Bardaiṣān was aware of the existence of Christians in Bactria. The word translated by Bactrians is in Syriac *Ḳaishānāye*, or the Kushans about whom Drouin writes:[3] "Les Kouchans ou Yue-tchi arrivèrent en Sogdiane, puis conquirent la Bactriane vers 129 de notre ère. Ils pénétrèrent dans l'Inde sous le nom de Kouchans

[1] Sachau's *Syr. Rechtsbücher*, iii. 1914, p. 209.

[2] *Book of the Laws* (in *Pat. Syr.*), ii. 607.

[3] *Mémoire sur les Huns Ephtalites* in *Museon*, 1895 (quoted on p. 589).

qui est celui d'une de leurs principales tribus (Kao-tchang ou Kouei-tchang). Ils furent subjugués au cinquième siècle par les Huns Ephtalites ou Huns Blancs." Parker[1] also makes mention of the Yueh-Chi, whose headquarters he places in Afghanistan, to the East of the Arsacids. The country of the Kushans, *Baith Kaishān*, is also mentioned in the Gnostic "Hymn of the Soul," found in the *Acts of Thomas*,[2] and written most probably in about A.D. 180-196.

For further details concerning the migrations and the conquests of the Yueh-Chi, see E. J. Rapson in *Cambridge History of India*, 1922, i. 563-592, especially p. 565 and p. 583. The two above scholars have been quoted because their works are omitted (apparently by oversight) in the otherwise excellent "Bibliography" of the *Cambridge History*, pp. 686-687.

We must also allude under this section to the explicit statement of the Syriac work entitled *Doctrine of the Apostles* edited from a fifth-sixth century MS. of the British Museum by many scholars, notably in 1864 by W. Cureton. The work itself cannot be much later than A.D. 250. On pp. 34-35 of the text it is asserted that the country of the Gilanians and that of Gog and Magog first received ecclesiastical ordination from the missionary called Aggai, a disciple of Addai, towards the beginning of the second century, say about A.D. 120-140. The readers of this study will be made aware of the fact that in Syriac literature the words Gog and Magog refer to the Turks and Tartars. We will not discuss here the question whether Aggai evangelised or not the countries of Central Asia, but we do maintain that the author of the *Doctrine*, whoever he was, knew about 250, as Bardaiṣān knew about 196, of the existence of Christians among the Gilanians on the Caspian Sea, and among the peoples of Turkic stock on the Oxus. See also Barhebraeus (*Chron. Eccl.*) ii. 15.

(*b*)

In about A.D. 498 the Sasanian king Ḳawad took twice refuge with the Hephtalite Huns and Turks, where he found Christians who helped him to reconquer his throne :—

"And Ḳubād escaped and went to the country of the Turks on account of the close friendship that he had contracted with the king

[1] *A Thousand Years of the Tartars*, pp. 34-36.

[2] Bedjan, *Acta Martyrum et Sanctorum*, iii. p. 111.

of the Turks when he had repaired to him in his father's lifetime. He asked the Turkish king for help, and the latter despatched an army with him to his country, and he dethroned Zamasp after a reign of two years. He killed some Magians, and incarcerated many others. He was benevolent towards the Christians, because a company of them rendered service to him on his way to the king of the Turks." [1]

This laconic historical information of a Nestorian writer is supplemented by a contemporary of Ḳawad, a well-informed Jacobite author who was writing in A.D. 555.[2] His text, which informs us that the Turks had learned the art of writing in their own language as early as about 550, is important and begins thus :—

"The Huns [3] more than twenty years ago learned the art of writing in their own language. I shall record the occasion of this event, which has been inspired by God, as I heard it from reliable people : John of Resh'aina, who was in the monastery of Isḥāḳonai, near Amed, and Thomas the tanner, who forcibly joined in the flight of Ḳawad from Persia into the country of the Huns, a little more than fifty years ago. They remained there more than thirty years, and married and had children there. They returned in our time, and in a vivid speech they narrated what follows." The document which is too long to translate in full proceeds to narrate that an angel appeared to the Bishop of Arran,[4] called Ḳaradusaṭ, and ordered him to repair to the numerous Byzantine captives among the Turks, and to the Turks themselves, in order to baptise them, ordain priests for them, and administer to them the Holy Eucharist. Four other priests accompanied them as missionaries, and the daily food of all seven consisted of seven loaves of bread and a jar of water. It was they who taught the Turks the art of writing in the Turkish language, and evangelised and baptised a considerable number of them. They lived with them seven years. In that time Probus, the messenger of the Roman Emperor Justinian, was sent on a special mission to the

[1] *Chronique de Seert*, in *Patr. Orient.*, vii. 128; cf. Tabari, *Annales*, I, 2, 887. Ḳawad's flight to the Turks is told at some length by Joshua the Stylite (about 507) in his Syriac *Chronicle*, pp. 18-19 of the text (edit. Wright).

[2] In *C.S.C.O.*, 3rd series, vol. vi. pp. 215-218.

[3] Old Styriac name of the Western Turks.

[4] About this Nestorian Bishopric see below.

country of the Turks, and seeing everything with his own eyes, he was astonished at what God had accomplished through his servants. On his way back he sent to them from the nearest town of the Empire thirty mules laden with flour, wine, oil, linen, and all the requisites of a Church vestry.

Their missionary labours were soon after shared by a practical Armenian Bishop who taught those Christian Turks how to plant vegetables and sow corn, and in the time of the writer he was still living among them. The grace of God touched also Ḳawad himself, the king of the Persians, who gave up eating unclean meat, and greatly honoured Joseph, who was a physician by profession, before becoming Patriarch of the Nestorians in 552.

On the two thousand Christian virgins selected for the Turks by the Sasanian king Chosrau I. see John of Ephesus's *Ecclesiastical History* (Payne-Smith, p. 387 *sq.*), and on the trouble the Turks often engendered between Romans and Persians, see *ibid.* p. 424 *sq.* Cf. also *Chronicon Anonymum* (in *C.S.C.O.*), i. 206.

About some aspects of the Hephthalite Huns and their wars with the Sasanians, see Blochet, *Introduction à l'histoire des Mongols*, pp. 211-214, where, however, no reference is made to the contemporary and important Syriac sources; and Nöldeke's well-known *Geschichte der Perser* (1879), pp. 53, 99, 158, 167, 250 *sqq.* and 269; cf. also Zacharias Rhetor in *C.S.C.O.*, i. 21 *sq.* and 98.

(*c*)

In A.D. 549, at the request of the Hephthalite or White Huns inhabiting the regions of Bactria, and those of both banks of the Oxus, the Nestorian Patriarch Aba I. sent a Bishop for all the Christians of his dominions :—

"After a short time Haphtar[1] Khudai sent a priest as a messenger to the King of Kings (Chosrau Anushirwān), and the Haphtrāye,[2] who were Christians, wrote also a letter to the holy Patriarch (Aba I.) requesting him to ordain as Bishop to all the kingdom of the Haphtrāye the priest who was sent from their country. When the priest saw the King of Kings, and the latter learned the nature of the mission on which he was sent, he was astonished to hear it, and

[1] The Syriac name for *Hephtalites.*

amazed at the power of Jesus, and at the fact that even the Christian Haphtrāye counted the Patriarch as their head and administrator. He therefore ordered him to go and adorn the Church as was customary on such occasions, and to ordain Bishop the man whom Haphtar Khudai had sent to him. On the following day the Church was adorned, and the Haphtrian priest was ordained Bishop for the Haphtrians, and joy increased with the people of the Lord."[1]

The extent to which Christianity had penetrated among these Turks may be gauged from the fact that in A.D. 581 those among them who were taken prisoners by the Byzantine Greeks had crosses on their forehead.[2] The crosses were pricked in black dots, and the Turks said that many years before, when a pestilence was ravaging the country, Christians had suggested to them to do this, and by it the pestilence had been averted. The use of the cross by the Nestorian Turks as a talisman is attested by Marco Polo (i. 343, edit. Yule-Cordier) and Friar William (Rockhill, *ibid.* pp. 104, 191, 193). See also in this connection the Syrian historians John of Ephesus (3rd part, book vi. ch. xxii.) and Michael the Syrian (ii. 314, and especially iii. 151, edit. Chabot).

(*d*)

In about A.D. 644 history makes mention of the conversion of large communities of Turks, thanks to the efforts and the zeal of Elijah, Metropolitan of Merw :—

"And Elijah, Metropolitan of Merw, converted a large number of Turks. . . . About this Elijah, Metropolitan of Merw, it is related that when travelling in the countries situated beyond the border line (of the river Oxus) he was met by a king who was going to fight another king. Elijah endeavoured with a long speech to dissuade him from the fight, but the king said to him, 'If thou showest to me a sign similar to those shown by the priests of my gods, I shall believe in thy God.' And the king ordered the priests of the demons who were accompanying him, and they invoked the demons whom they

[1] *Histoire de Mar Aba.* (edit. Bedjan), pp. 266-269.

[2] Theophylactus Simocatta's "History of the Emperor Maurice," quoted by Rockhill (*in op. infrà laud.*), p. 142, and in *Cathay*, 1915, i. 115 (edit. Yule-Cordier). The intercourse between Byzantine Emperors and Turkish Khāns is well illustrated by Menander Protector in *Cathay* (*ibid.* i. 205 *sq.*).

were worshipping, and immediately the sky was covered with clouds, and a hurricane of wind, thunder, and lightning followed. Elijah was then moved by divine power, and he made the sign of the heavenly cross, and rebuked the unreal thing that the rebellious demons had set up, and it forthwith disappeared completely. When the king saw what Saint Elijah did, he fell down and worshipped him, and he was converted with all his army. The saint took them to a stream, baptised all of them, ordained for them priests and deacons, and returned to his country." [1]

(*e*)

In about A.D. 781 Timothy, the Nestorian Patriarch, wrote in his letter to the Maronites, that another king of the Turks had become Christian with all his people :—

"The king of the Turks, with nearly all (the inhabitants of) his country, has left his ancient idolatry, and has become Christian, and he has requested us in his letters to create a Metropolitan for his country ; and this we have done." [2] Further, in one of his letters to Rabban Sergius, the same Timothy says that he has ordained a Bishop for the Turks, and that he was going to ordain one for Tibet :—

"In these days the Holy Spirit has anointed a Metropolitan for the Turks, and we are preparing to consecrate another one for the Tibetans." [3]

Finally, in another letter to Sergius, the illustrious Patriarch clearly states that in his time "many monks crossed the sea and went to the Indians and the Chinese with only a rod and a scrip," [4] and apprises his correspondent of the death of the Metropolitan of China. [5]

(*f*)

Thomas of Marga writes that the same indefatigable Patriarch chose more than four score of monks, some of whom he ordained

[1] *Chronica Minora*, in *Corp. Script. Christ. Orient.*, pp. 34-35 of the text which was written about A.D. 680.

[2] The letter is not yet published. I read it in a MS. Cf. J. Labourt's *De Timotheo I Nestorianorum Patriarcha*, p. 43.

[3] *Oriens Christianus*, i. 308.

[4] *Timothei Epistolæ*, i. p. 107 of the text (in *C.S.C.O.*).

[5] *Ibid.* p. 109.

Bishops, and sent them to convert the heathens of the Far East ; and narrates the exploits of Shubḥa-lîshō', Metropolitan of the Dailamites of the South-Eastern parts of the Caspian Sea :—

"(These Bishops) were ordained by the holy Catholicos Timothy the Patriarch to the countries of the savage peoples, who were devoid of every understanding and civilisation. No missionaries and sowers of truth had till then gone to their regions, and the teaching of the Gospel of our Saviour had not yet been preached to them ; but why should I say the teaching of the Christ, our Lord, while they had not even received, like the Jews and the rest of the Gentiles (i.e. Muslims), the knowledge of God, Creator and Administrator of the worlds, but were worshipping trees, graven wood, beasts, fish, reptiles, birds and such-like, along with the worship of fire and stars. These were the Bishops who preached the teaching of Christ in those countries of the Dailamites and Gilānians, and the rest of the savage peoples beyond them, and planted in them the light of the truth of the Gospel of our Lord. . . . They evangelised them and they baptised them, worked miracles and showed prodigies, and the news of their exploits reached the farthest points of the East. You may learn all these clearly from the letter which some merchants and secretaries of the kings, who had penetrated as far as there for the sake of commerce and of affairs of State, wrote to (the Patriarch) Mar Timothy."[1]

In another place the same historian relates how Bishop Shubḥa-lîshō' was ordained by Timothy, and describes his fitness for the task set to him, which was that of evangelising the primitive peoples inhabiting the countries lying beyond Central Asia, and says that he was versed not only in Syriac, but also in Arabic and Persian. He dilates on the great number of miracles which God performed through him, and continues :—

"He taught and baptised many towns and numerous villages, and brought them to the teaching of the divine life. He built churches, and set up in them priests and deacons, and singled out some brethren who were missionaries with him to teach them psalms and canticles of the Spirit. And he himself went deep inland to the farthest end of the East, in the work of the great evangelisation that he was doing among pagans, Marcionites, Manichæans, and other kinds of beliefs

[1] Thomas of Marga, *Liber Superiorum*, pp. 261-262 (edit. Bedjan).

and abominations, and he sowed the sublime light of the teaching of the Gospel, the source of life and peace."[1]

The enthusiasm of the historian is explained by the fact that he was contemporary with the events he was narrating. Further references to the same evangelisation may be seen in his book on pp. 275-281. He ends his account as follows : "The bread of those countries was made of rice, because the blessed cereals wheat and barley are not found there, but only rice and other kinds of similar grains. We learned this from the mouth of Mar Yahb Alāha, of good memory. The two old men Ḥnānishō' and Elishā' used to tell me that (the Saint) related that when he started to come back, and reached the holy Ḥabbība, Metropolitan of the city of Ray, he ate wheat bread, and because of that he fell gravely ill, owing to the fact that he was used in those countries to eat bread of rice only."

On page 245 the same historian mentions among the Bishops ordained in his Monastery of Beith 'Ābé, Elijah, Bishop of Mūḳān, and David, Metropolitan of China. Thomas, who was writing about 840, adds immediately after the mention of the name of the above Metropolitan, that the information concerning him is drawn from the letters of the Patriarch Timothy, who died in 823.

(*g*)

Māri informs us that Timothy converted the Ḳāghān (king) of the Turks, and other kings, and that he was in correspondence with them :—

"And Timothy converted to the (Christian) faith the Khāḳān of the Turks and other kings, from whom he received letters, and he instructed many in Christian doctrine."[2]

(*h*)

In about A.D. 1009, 'Abdishō', Metropolitan of Merw, wrote to the Nestorian Patriarch, John, informing him that about two hundred thousand Turks and Mongols had embraced Christianity, and asked him concerning the kind of food they were to eat in Lent, as no food suitable for that Fast was to be found in their country :—

"In that time 'Abdīshō', Metropolitan of Merw, one of the towns

[1] Thomas of Marga, *Liber Superiorum*, pp. 269-271.
[2] *Book of the Tower*, p. 73 (text), and 64 of the transl. (edit. Gismondi).

of Khurāsān, wrote and informed the Catholicos that while the king of a people called Keraits, Eastern Turks inhabiting the region of the North-East,[1] was hunting in one of the high mountains of his country, he was overcome by a violent snow-storm, and wandered hopelessly out of the way. When he lost all hope of salvation, a saint appeared to him in vision and said to him, 'If you believe in Christ, I will lead you to the right direction, and you will not die here.' When he promised him that he would become a lamb in the Christian sheepfold, he directed him and led him to salvation ; and when he reached his tents in safety, he summoned the Christian merchants who were there, and discussed with them the question of faith, and they answered him that this could not be accomplished except through baptism. He took a Gospel from them, and lo he is worshipping it every day ; and now he has summoned me to repair to him, or to send him a priest to baptise him. He also made enquiries from me concerning fasting, and said to me, 'Apart from meat and milk, we have no other food ; how could we then fast' ; he also told me that the number of those who were converted with him reached two hundred thousand. The Catholicos wrote then to the Metropolitan, and told him to send two persons, a priest and a deacon, with all the requisites of an altar, to go and baptise all those who were converted, and to teach them Christian habits. As to the Fast of Lent, they should abstain in it from meat, but they should be given permission to drink milk, if, as they say, Lent food is not found in their country."[2]

Barhebraeus makes also mention of this conversion in his general history under A.H. 398 as follows :—

"In this very year a nation from the nations of the Turks inhabiting the interior of the country towards the East, called Kerit, believed in Christ, and were instructed in the faith and baptised through a miracle that happened to their king."[3]

We must here state that the legend of "Prester John," which was so widely diffused in Europe in the Middle Ages, is closely connected with the above Keraits, because "John" was given as their king. As it has been often explained "John" in Syriac

[1] The habitat of these Karaites was near the river Orkhon and lake Baikal. See below.

[2] Barhebraeus, *Chron. Eccles.*, iii. pp. 279-280 (edit. Lamy).

[3] *Chron. Syr.*, p. 204 (edit. Bedjan), cf. Assemani, *B.O.*, iv. 486.

"Yoḥannan" may be a falsification of "Ung-Khan," name of one of the Kerait rulers, and Barhebraeus[1] clearly identifies the mythical "John" with the historical "Ung." His proper name was called Tuli by the Chinese, and Ṭoghrul by the Persian historians, but the Kin Sovereign of Northern China had conferred on him the title of Wang (= King) from which the slightly corrupted cognomen of *Ung*.[2]

The Keraits lived on the Orkhon and the Tula, S.E. of lake Baikal.[3]

(*i*)

Māri relates the same event, and gives additional details as follows :—

"A letter came (to the Patriarch) from 'Abdīshō', the Metropolitan of Merw, to the effect that an Archdeacon had become Muslim, and had turned his Church into a mosque ; but after some days canker invaded his limbs and he died, and the Church reverted to its former owners. The letter contained also the following fact :—

A king from the Turkish kings became Christian with two hundred thousand souls. The cause of this was that he lost his way when he went hunting, and while he was bewildered not knowing what to do, he saw the figure of a man who promised salvation to him. He asked him about his name, and he told him that it was Mar Sergius. He intimated to him to become Christian, and said to him, 'close your eyes,' and he closed them. When he opened them, he found himself in his camp. He was amazed at this, and he made inquiries concerning Christian religion, prayer, and book of canon-laws. He was taught the Lord's Prayer, *Lākhū Māra*,[4] and *Ḳaddīsha Alāha*.[4] The Bishop told also (the Patriarch) that he had written to him on the subject of his going to him, and that he was informed that his people were accustomed to eat only meat and milk. The king had set up a pavilion to take the place of an altar, in which was a cross and a Gospel, and named it after Mar Sergius, and he tethered a mare there, and he takes her milk and lays it on the Gospel and the

[1] *Chron. Syr.* p. 409 (edit. Bedjan).

[2] Yule-Cordier, in *Marco Polo* (*op. infrà. cit.*), i. 237.

[3] Rockhill, in *Journey of Rubruck* (*op. infrà. cit.*), p. 111.

[4] Prayers of the Nestorian Church. See *Breviarium Chaldaicum*, i., ii., iii. pp. 4 and 9 (edit. Bedjan).

cross, and recites over it the prayers which he has learned, and makes the sign of the Cross over it, and he and his people after him take a draught from it. The Metropolitan inquired from (the Patriarch) what was to be done with them as they had no wheat, and the latter answered him to endeavour to find them wheat and wine for Easter; as to abstinence, they should abstain at Lent from meat, and be satisfied with milk. If their habit was to take sour milk, they should take sweet milk as a change to their habit." [1]

This is evidently an allusion to the well-known sour milk of the Turks and Tartars. See about it Yule, in *Marco Polo*, i. 249, and Rockhill, in *William of Rubruck*, pp. 66-67 and the authorities quoted by them.

(*j*)

In their letters to the Patriarchs, the Nestorian Metropolitans of Central Asia do not write only on religious affairs, but a few of them describe also political events of first importance. Barhebraeus in his general history under A.H. 438 registers the following event:—

"In this year the Nestorian Metropolitan of Samarḳand sent a letter to the Catholicos, which was read also at the Court of the Caliph (in which it was written) that people resembling locusts by their numbers, had made a breach in the wall which separated Tibet from Khotan and which, according to old traditions, was fortified by Alexander the Great. They passed through it, and reached as far as Kashgar. There were seven kings, and with each one of them there were seven hundred thousand mounted troops. The name of their great king was Nāṣarat, which means "Governing by the command of God." They were half black like Indians; they did not wash their faces, neither did they comb their hair, but they fulled it like a felt rug and it served them as a shield. They ate sparingly of simple food, and were merciful and just, and their horses were carnivores." [2]

The extent to which Christianity had penetrated among those Mongols who in the Lower Middle Ages swept over Western Asia and Eastern Europe with such a lightning rapidity, is well illustrated by Barhebraeus, a contemporary, and often also an eye-witness of

[1] *Book of the Tower*, in the Life of John V., p. 100 of Gismondi's translation, cf. Assemani, *B.O.* iv. 484.

[2] Barhebraeus, *Chron. Syr.*, pp. 228-229 (edit. Bedjan), cf. Assemani, *B.O.*, iv. 487.

many incidents which he reports in his *Chron. Syr.* so often quoted in the previous pages. We will only refer here to the following incidents :—

About the Mongolian Emperor Guyūk, made famous in Europe by Friar John of Pian de Carpine, who in 1246 brought to him a letter from the Pope, Barhebraeus writes : "And Guyūk was a true Christian, and in his days the prestige of the numerous Christians of his dominions was very high.[1] His camp was full of Bishops, priests and monks" (p. 481, edit. Bedjan).—"And from the wives of Tūli Khan, their father, Dōḳūz Khātūn, the believing and the true Christian queen was given for marriage to Hūlāku, according to the habit of the Mongols. She enhanced the prestige of Christians in all the earth" (p. 491).—When Baghdad was taken by the Mongols, the Christians were spared death and torture (p. 505) because of "the magnanimity, the wisdom, and the marvellously high character of Hūlāku,"[2] whose figure has been blackened almost beyond recognition by some modern writers : "And in the year 1576 (A.D. 1265), at the beginning of Lent, Hūlāku, the King of Kings, left this world. There was no one who could be compared to him in wisdom, magnanimity, and marvellously high character. And in the summer days Dōḳūz Khātūn[3] also, the believing queen, died. The Christians of all the world greatly mourned the death of these two great luminaries and protagonists of Christian religion" (p. 521).—Another Christian queen who preceded the above Doḳūz Khātūn, and who was "a true believer like Helen," and "wisest of all," is Sarḳūti Bagi,[4] the wife of Tūli Khan, the son of Chingis Khan, and his successor to the throne of the Mongolian Empire. She was the niece of the Kerait

[1] Cf. Juwaini's *Jahān Gushā* (in Gibb Mem.), ii. 247-248, and see Rashīd's *Jāmi' at Tawārīkh* (*ibid.*) p. 273, where the Christian convictions of his successor Mangu Khan are clearly set forth in the following words, "a follower and a defender of the Religion of Jesus." The Christianism of Guyūk Khan himself is also attested by Rashīd, *ibid.* p. 249.

[2] Hūlāku judged by our ethical standards was doubtless cruel ; but our standards are not those of the Mongols, nor even those of the early Empires of Asia and Europe, including those founded or directed by men whom we call prophets. The testimony of a contemporary of Barhebraeus's standing cannot be entirely disregarded.

[3] About Doḳuz Khātūn, see Blochet in *Jāmi' at Tawārīkh* (Gibb Mem.), p. 200.

[4] See Rashīd's *Jāmi' at Tawārīkh* (*ibid.*), pp. 89 and 222, etc.

king Ung Khan, of the Prester John fame, and the mother of the following Princes and Emperors: Munga Khan, Ḳublai Khan, Hūlāku Khan, and Arig Bōga (pp. 465 and 488).

Page 481: the Christian Kaddak is the Grand Vizier of the Emperor Guyuk.[1]—P. 528: a monk becomes a Muslim, and on this occasion a great uproar arises between Christians and Muslims, and the Christians are helped by the Mongol governor of North Mesopotamia who was a Christian.—P. 529: the Christian Mongols help the Christian community of Arbel against the Muslims on the occasion of a procession with crosses and banners on Palm Sunday.—P. 535: the envoy of Ḳublai Khan is a Turkish Uighurian nobleman, who was a Christian.—P. 539: the queen Ḳutai Khātūn in order to put an end to a terribly cold weather, commands the Christians of Marāgha to resort to the ceremony of the blessing of the water, with spears ending in crosses.—Pp. 543 and 554: the Christians are given the Governorship of North Mesopotamia.—P. 547: the Emperor Abāḳa goes to Church on Easter Day.—P. 569: all clerks in Government Offices are to be either from the Christian or from the Jewish communities, and not from the Muslims.—P. 578: the Īl-Khān Arghūn sends the Rabban Ṣauma embassy spoken of below to seek an alliance with the Pope and the Christian kings of the West, in order to crush Islam.—P. 593: the Emperor Baidu, before becoming a Muslim, takes Christian sanctuaries and bells in his camp for the celebration of the Mass, and hangs a cross on his neck.

(*k*)

We come now to that most interesting book, "The History of Mar Yahb-Alāha" (*Deus dedit = Deo-datus*), which is of paramount importance for the history of Christianity in China, Turkestan, and Mongolia, in the thirteenth Christian century. It was published in Leipzig by Bedjan in 1888, and re-edited by him in 1895. The history is based on the following facts:—

A Christian, Ṣauma by name, was born in Peking in the first half of the thirteenth century, and on his attaining the age of manhood, he became a monk at the hands of Georges, the Nestorian Metropolitan of China; seven years later he left his native city in order to lead

[1] See Juwaini's *Jahān Gushā* i. 200-201, etc., and especially Rashid's *Jāmi' at Tawārīkh* (*ibid.*), p. 249.

more easily the life of a hermit, after which his soul was constantly aspiring; he was soon followed by another Christian, called Marcus, who was born in Kaushang in 1244, and who received the monastic garb at the hands of another Metropolitan called Nestorius. After having spent some time in their hermitage, they left together their native country to go to Jerusalem on pilgrimage, viâ Tangut, Kashgar, Ṭūs, and Marāgha. Marcus is then ordained Metropolitan of China, under the name of Yahb-Alāha, and his friend and colleague Ṣauma is nominated Visitor-General. After two years, Yahb-Alāha becomes Patriarch of the Nestorians, and during his long term of office which lasted thirty-six years, he saw eight Mongol Il-Khans succeeding one another: Abaḳa, Aḥmad, Arghūn, Gaikhātu, Baidu, Ghāzān, Uljaitu, and Bahādur Khan.

In 1287-8 the Emperor Arghūn and the Patriarch sent an embassy headed by Ṣauma to the Pope Nicholas IV. and the Christian kings of Europe,[1] in order to form a mutual alliance against the Muslims. The highly interesting narrative of the journey undertaken by this embassy sheds great rays of light on the glorious Nestorian Christianity at the time of its greatest expansion, just before it received the death blow which reduced it to a mere sect of not more than a few hundred thousand souls. From this period the Church gradually declined until in our own days it has shrunk to a miserable community of about 40,000 refugees, the bulk of whom have settled round the city of Mosul, in the new Kingdom of 'Irāḳ.

(*l*)

It is not our intention to refer here in full to the account of Western travellers and explorers, but in order to illustrate the narrative of some Syrian historians, and corroborate the information of Syrian Synods, we cannot resist the temptation to refer, very shortly, at least to a few Western travellers of outstanding merit and importance, such as the immortal Marco Polo, and the Friars William of Rubruck, and John of Pian de Carpine.

The former speaks of Nestorians in (*a*) Kashgar, where they are numerous and "have churches of their own";[2] (*b*) in Samarḳand,

[1] The arrival of the embassy in England is found on pp. 72-73 of Bedjan's second edition.

[2] *Marco Polo*, i. p. 182. (We refer to H. Yule's edition, 1903, with notes by Cordier.)

where the uncle of the Emperor Ḳublai became Christian, and on this occasion the Christians built a new great Church in honour of John the Baptist (i. 184-185); (*c*) in Yarkand (i. p. 187); (*d*) in Tangut (i. 203); (*e*) in Chingintalas (i. 212); (*f*) in Sukchur, where about half of the inhabitants belonged to their Church (i. 217); (*g*) in Kanchou, where they had "three very fine Churches"; (*h*) in Erguil and Sinju (i. 274); (*i*) in Calachan, where they had "fine Churches;" (*j*) in Tenduc, where "the rule of the province is in the hands of the Christians" (i. 284); (*k*) in Cathay (i. 285); (*l*) in Yachi (ii. 66); (*m*) in Cacanfu; (*n*) in Yangchau, where there were three Churches (ii. 154); and finally in Chinghianfu (ii. 177).

Friar William finds them also in nearly all the countries which he traverses; he meets with them in the country of Karakhata, where he noticed that the Turkish people called Nayman had for King a Nestorian;[1] the Emperor Sartach "has Nestorian priests around him who strike a board and chant their offices" (*ibid.* p. 116); "the Nestorians among the Uigurs (Eastern Turks) perform their services in the latter's language and write books in those letters; in all their towns is found a mixture of Nestorians" (*ibid.* p. 141); "the Uigurs have adopted the alphabet of the Nestorians" (*ibid.* p. 150; this sentence is from Pian de Carpine); "the Nestorians are Mongol scribes" (*ibid.* p. 150); "In fifteen cities of Cathay there are Nestorians, and they have an episcopal see in the city called Segin" (*ibid.* p. 157); "about three leagues from Cailac we found a village entirely of Nestorians" (*ibid.* p. 159); "the secretary of the Emperor Mangu, Bulgai by name, was a Nestorian" (*ibid.* p. 168); "the Emperor had his interpreter, a Nestorian" (*ibid.* p. 173): in certain holy days in the ecclesiastical calendar, "first come the Nestorian priests with their apparel, and they pray for the Emperor and bless his cup"; "and the Emperor sent one of the blessed loaves to the Emperor's son and to one of his younger brothers, who was being brought up by a Nestorian, and he knows the Gospels" (*ibid.* pp. 212-213); "and the Nestorians gave me the use of their baptistery in which was an altar; their Patriarch had sent them from Baghdad a quadrangular

[1] *The Journey of William of Rubruck . . . with two accounts of . . . John of Pian de Carpine*, translated by W. W. Rockhill, in "Hakluyt Society's" publications, No. iv. of the second series.

skin for an *antimensium*, and it had been anointed with chrism" (*ibid.* p. 215).

The other European travellers of the Middle Ages should not detain us long. "There is a kingdom twenty days' journey from Cathay of which the king and all the inhabitants are Christians, but heretics, being said to be Nestorians" (Nicolo Conti in *Cathay*, ii. 165-166).—"And in the great city of Iamzai (Yang-chau-fu) there are three churches of the Nestorians" (Friar Odoric, *Cathay*, ii. 210).—"These Nestorians are more than thirty thousand, dwelling in the said empire of Cathay, and are passing rich people. . . . They have very handsome and devoutly ordered churches, with crosses and images in honour of God and the saints. They hold sundry offices under the said emperor, and have great privileges from him; so that it is believed that if they would agree and be at one with the Minor Friars, they would convert the whole country and the emperor likewise to the true faith" (John de Cora, *Cathay*, iii. 102).—"The Uighurs were Christians of the sect of the Nestorians" (Pian de Carpine in *Friar William; passim*).—"The Nestorians . . . have grown so powerful in Cathay that they will not allow a Christian of another ritual to have ever so small a chapel" (John of Monte Corvino, *Cathay*, iii. 46).

It is clear from all the above quotations and from some other data given below that the majority of the two powerful divisions of the Turco-Tartar race: the Uighurs and the Keraits[1] were Christians. The Gospel of Christ had also penetrated another powerful confederacy of Turco-Tartar tribes, the Naimans, who comprised nine powerful clans,[2] the greater part of whom lived in the mountains of Tarbagatai, the Upper Irtish, and other places on the Chinese frontier; the remainder on the Upper Ishim and the neighbouring countries. Rubruck expressly stated that they were Christians: "A people called Naiman who were Nestorian Christians,"[3] and Persian historians apply to them the epithet *Tarsa* which, as stated on p. 322, refers to Christians.[4]

[1] Rashid (d'Ohsson, i. 48) erroneously states that the Keraits were converted to Christianity in the time of Chingis Khan. See above, p. 309.

[2] Howorth's *History*, ii. 8; d'Ohsson, i. 167. In 1212 a Naiman prince of Nestorian Christianity "raised himself up to be king and seized the throne." Rubruck, *ibid.* p. 110.

[3] Rockhill, *ibid.* p. 110.

[4] *Ibid.* 17.

A fourth agglomeration of tribes who were probably half-Christians are the Merkites, a nomadic people of Turkish stock with a possible infusion of Mongol blood. They were divided into four main sections, and lived on the lower Selinga and its feeders.[1] Their Christianity is attested by Rubruck.[2] They are to be distinguished from the Keraits, and Pian de Carpine[3] even believes them to be different from the Mekrites, who jointly with the Merkites formed the four "nations" who once constituted the Mongol stock.

On p. 337 we have also given evidence to the effect that a fifth agglomeration of Turkish tribes, the Uriyān-gaḳit, were Christians, and had in 1298 a Christian queen.

We exclude from the purview of our enquiry the Chinese and Mohammedan historians, but we cannot refrain from quoting an author of exceptional authority, to wit, 'Ali ibn Rabban aṭ-Ṭabari, the well-informed physician and table-guest of the Caliph Mutawakkil (847-861). In a memorable sentence he compares the Christianity of those Eastern Turks who form the subject of the references of some of our historians and Synods, to that of the Armenians, of the Greeks, and of the Franks of Europe, . . . "and kindled it (the war) with spears and swords as far as the countries of the Greeks, of the Franks, of the tent-dwelling Turanians, and of the Armenians. Outside these countries what Christians are to be found in the country of the Turks except a small and despicable quantity of Nestorians, scattered among the nations?"[4]

Here the Muslim apologist and the ex-secretary of the heroic but unfortunate Māzyār of Tabaristan apparently draws a distinction between Turanians and Turks. The latter, who were mostly Muslims, he simply styles "Turks," but to the former, because of their Christianity, he applies the derisive epithet of "Turanians," a name of which a nationalist "Iranian" Persian would readily make use in speaking of the Turks.

2. Synods and Bishoprics.

We will enumerate here the Bishoprics of the countries bordering on the river Oxus. If a town is considered to be worth promoting to a

[1] D'Ohsson, *Histoire*, i. 54; Howorth, *ibid.* i. 22, 698.
[2] Rockhill, *ibid.* p. 111. [3] *Ibid.* p. 112.
[4] *Book of Religion and Empire*, p. 156 of my edition.

Bishopric, or even an Archbishopric, it is hardly possible to deny the existence in it or round it of a rather considerable number of Christians. We cannot here attempt to give even a rough estimate of the number of Christians who in ancient times inhabited the zone extending from about the centre of modern Persia as far as the end of the continent of Asia, and with the sources at our disposal such an estimate would be well nigh impossible, but there seems to be no exaggeration in asserting that there were Christians scattered in almost all the innumerable districts of this immense territory, and that they were in rather considerable strength in some specified towns or localities. Their number must have varied according to the importance of a place as a centre of commerce or as a highway to be constantly trodden under the feet of camels, mules, or horses. We will divide this section into two distinct geographical groups : (1) the regions lying on the Western banks of the river ; (2) those lying on the Eastern banks. The Bishoprics in the first section are given in the alphabetical order :—

A.

Western Banks of the River.

Abīward or **Bāward**, the district lying north-west of Khurāsān on the edge of the Merw desert. A Bishop John is mentioned for it in the Synod of Joseph in 554 (p. 366).[1] The diocese embraced also the neighbouring town of Shahr-Phīrūz.

Abrashahr, the district of Khurāsān in which the more modern town of Naishapur is built. Abrashahr is also called Iran Shahr. A Bishop, David, is mentioned for it in the Synod of Dadishō‘ in 424 (p. 285), and another called Yoḥannis in the Synod of Babai in 497 (pp. 310, 311, 316). In this last year the see was enlarged so as to include also Ṭūs. It is to be distinguished from another *Abrashahr* better known under the name of Hamshahrah in the Mūḳān. See Le Strange's *Lands of the Eastern Caliphate*, p. 176.

Amul,[2] in Tabaristan, north of Damawand. A Bishop, Sūrīn, is mentioned for it in the Synod of Joseph in 554 (p. 366).

[1] Unless otherwise stated all the references are to the *Synodicon Orientale*.

[2] To be distinguished from the Amul, on the left bank of the Oxus, about 120 miles to the north-east of Merw (see Le Strange's *Lands of the East. Caliph.*, pp. 403-404, etc.).

Arran, the region north of the rivers Araxes and Kur, west of the Caspian Sea. A Bishop is mentioned for it in the Synod of Yahb-Alāha in 420 (p. 276, cf. also p. 619).

Badīsi, or **Bādhgīs**, a district situated north of Herat. It was the residence of the Hephthalite Turkish Kings. A Bishop, Gabriel, is mentioned for it in the Synod of Ishō'-Yahb in 585 (p. 423).

Bist (or **Bust**), a town in Sijistan on the river Helmund. A Bishop, Sergius, is mentioned for it in the Synod of Aba in 544 (pp. 343-344).

Būshanj, a town west of Herat, on the Harī-rūd. A Bishop, Ḥabīb, is mentioned for it in the Synod of Isho'-Yahb in 585.

Dailūmāyé (Beith), was a province near the Caspian Sea, and it was a Bishopric as early as A.D. 225.[1] Sachau[2] believes that this information may possibly refer to Dailamistan, which according to Yāḳūt (*Mu'jam*, ii. 711, edit. Wüstenfeld) was a village near Shahrzūr, which served as a halting place to the Sasanian kings.

Farah, a town in Sijistan near the river of this name. A Bishop, Yazd-Afrīd, is mentioned for it in the Synod of Aba in 544 (pp. 343-344). The diocese was joined then to that of Ḳash, another town situated south-east of Farah.

Herat, a town in Khurāsān, north-west of modern Afghanistan. A Bishop, Yazdoi, is mentioned for it in the Synod of Dadīshō' in 424; another of its Bishops, Gabriel, is found in the Synod of Aḳāḳ in 486; a third Bishop, Yazdād, attends the Synod of Babai in 497; and a fourth Bishop, Gabriel, is in the Synod of Isho'-Yahb, in 585 (pp. 285, 299, 301, 311, 423, cf. p. 620).

Jilān (or **Gilān**), province of the south-west coast of the Caspian Sea. A Bishop, Sūrīn, is mentioned for it in the Synod of Joseph in 554 (p. 366). We must here refer to the eighteen martyrs of Jilān, who suffered martyrdom on the 12th April, 351, under Sapor II. (Bedjan, *Acta Mart.* iv. 166-170). According to Barhebraeus (ii. 15) the Gilanians were converted by the Apostle Addai.

Jurjān, province of the south-east coast of the Caspian Sea. A Bishop, Abraham, is mentioned for it in the Synod of Bābai in 497; another Bishop, Z'ōra, is found in the Synod of Ezechiel in 576 (pp. 310, 311, 316, 368).

Ḳādistan, a district in the neighbourhood of Herat. A Bishop, Gabriel, is mentioned for it in the Synod of Isho'-Yahb in 585 (p. 423).

Khamlikh, a town of the Khazars in Hyrcania, on the Caspian Sea. The Bishopric is mentioned by 'Amr,[3] and Gismondi has wrongly printed it

[1] Mshīha-Zkha, in my *Sources Syriaques*, i. 30.
[2] *Ausbreitung*, p. 9.
[3] *De Pat. Nest. Comm.* (edit. Gismondi), pp. 126, 132.

as Ḥalaḥ and Ḥalīḥ. The correction is due to Sachau,[1] who rightly refers to Yaḳūt, *Geographical Dictionary*, ii. 437.

Merw, a celebrated town north of Khurāsan. A Bishop, Bar Shabba,[2] is mentioned for it in the Synod of Dadīshō' in 424; another Bishop, Parūmai, is found in the Synod of Aḳāḳ in 486; a third Bishop, John, was in the Synod of Babai in 497; a fourth Bishop, called David, was in the Synod of Aba in 544, and in that of Joseph in 554; and a fifth Bishop, Gregory, is mentioned in the Synod of Ishō'-Yahb in 585 (pp. 285, 306, 310, 315, 328, 332, 366, 367, 423).

Merw-ar-Rūd, a town built by the Sasanian King Bahram IV. at about four days' journey south of Merw. A Bishop, Theodore, is mentioned for it in the Synod of Joseph in 544 (p. 366).

Ray, a very important town formerly situated north-east of the Jibāl Province, about thirty miles south-east of modern Teheran. A Bishop, David, is mentioned for it in the Synod of Dadīshō' in 424; another Bishop, Joseph, attended the Synod of Aḳāḳ in 486, and of Babai in 497; a third Bishop, Daniel, is mentioned in the Synod of Aba in 544.

Rukhut, a town in Sijistan. A Bishop is mentioned for it in the Synod of Aba in 544 (pp. 343-344).

Sijistan, the well-known province situated in our days in modern Afghanistan. A Bishop, Afrīd, is mentioned for it in the Synod of Dadīsho, in 424; other Bishops, Yazd-Afrīd and Sergius, are found in the Synod of Aba in 544; a third Bishop, called Kurmah, attended the Synod of Ezechiel in 576 (pp. 285, 339, 343, 368).

Ṭūs, ancient capital of Khurāsan; its ruins are seen at about fifteen miles north-west of Mashhad. A Bishop, Yoḥannis, is mentioned for it in the Synod of Babai in 497 (pp. 311, 316). From this date the diocese comprised also the town of Abrashahr.

Zarang, an important town in Sijistan. A Bishop, Yazd-Afrīd, is mentioned for it in the Synod of Aba in 544 (pp. 343-344).

B.

Eastern Banks of the River.

We include under this head East and West Turkestan of our days, Mongolia, Manchuria, North China, and South-Eastern parts of Siberia. Unfortunately the Synods of the Nestorian Church do

[1] *Ausbreitung*, p. 22.

[2] See about him Māri, *Book of the Tower*, p. 23, and *Chronique de Seert*, ii. 253-258.

not bring us any help in this part of our research, because, owing to the long distance that separated the above countries from the centre of the Patriarchate, there was a moral impossibility for their Bishops to attend the ecclesiastical assemblies with their colleagues whose diocese were nearer the Sasanian, and at a later date, the Abbasid, capital, where the Patriarch resided and held as unlimited a spiritual power as that wielded by any Pope of the Middle Ages ; indeed, 'Abdīshō' informs us in his *Synodical Canons* (cap. xix.), that the Metropolitans of India, China, and Samarḳand were, owing to long distances, exempted from attending the General Synods of the Church ; instead of their personal attendance they had to write a letter of submission to the Patriarch once every six years, in order to inform him of the spiritual and moral needs of their dioceses.[1] The official Acts of Councils being thus by necessity deficient in the information which would highly interest modern scholars, we will turn our attention to the historians of these Councils, the general historians, and the official correspondence that passed from time to time between the Patriarch and the very remote Bishops or Archbishops of those regions.

We believe that it was this immense geographical distance that was the cause of the slight divergences in the religious outlook, and even in some minor points of dogma, that separate the official Christianity of the Eastern Church from that which one finds in the Christian monuments unearthed by the explorers of the last half century. These differences extend even to liturgical prayers attributed to no less important Fathers than Theodore of Mopsuestia,[2] and Narsai.[3] By force of circumstances, those far-off Bishops were left more or less to themselves ; and cast off from the rest of their religious brethren of the West they had to manage their spiritual and ecclesiastical affairs to the best of their ability.

The Syriac writers of the more civilised regions of the Sasanian Empire had often only vague ideas of the ethnographical characteristics of the peoples inhabiting the far-off regions beyond the Oxus, and their geographical acquaintance with the nature of the country seems also to

[1] Cf. Assemani, *B.O.*, iii. 347, and iv. 439.

[2] See our *Synopsis of Christian Doctrine according to Theodore of Mopsuestia*, 1920.

[3] See the introduction to our edition of his Works : *Narsai Homiliæ et Carmina*, 1904, vol. i.

have been deficient in more points than one. In this respect they resembled many of their Muslim successors and pupils in Greek sciences, whose knowledge of those regions is often summed up in the vague phrase *ma warā, annahr*, "on the other side of the river" Oxus. To our knowledge, no Syriac writer has even mentioned by name the Mongols, till the Lower Middle Ages, i.e. till the time when they swept over the whole civilised world, and conquered it with a rapidity unparalleled in the annals of history. Everything beyond the Oxus is generally referred by Syrian historians to the less remote Turks and Huns with whom they had more intimate intercourse. The writer of the present document singles himself out from almost all other writers who preceded and followed him down to the Mongol invasion, by once applying to them the more accurate ethnological appellation of *Tatar*, which some ignorant people of Europe transformed in later generations into *Tartars* from tartarus, "hell" (cf. the well-known sentence of Matthew Paris). In the Mongol Empire the Christians were sometimes known under the name of *Tarsa*, but more generally under that of *Arkägün*.[1]

Apart from the information furnished by the present document, the oldest references found in Syriac literature to the existence of Bishoprics in Turkestan is that recorded in the "Life of Mar Aba" which we have already quoted, and which goes as far back as A.D. 549. Unfortunately the historian does not give us the name of the town where the newly ordained Bishop resided.

The late compilers of juridical decisions of the Synods refer to the dioceses situated beyond the Oxus simply by the words "Metropolitan of the Turks," i.e. Turkestan. This Metropolitan must presumably have had many Suffragan Bishops under him. This view is rendered probable by the fact that the "Metropolitan of the Turks" was in the rank of precedence counted as Xth among the high Metropolitans of the Nestorian Church, who had under their jurisdiction about one hundred and eighty Bishops, and took precedence over the Metropolitans of Razikāyé (comprising Ray, Ḳum, and Ḳāshān), that of Heriwāné, i.e. of Herat, that of Armenia, and finally that of China (Ṣīn and Māṣīn) and Java,[2] who was the fifteenth in rank.

[1] Pelliot, in *T'oung Pao*, 1914, p. 636. In the *Jāmi' at-Tawārīkh of Rashīd ad-Dīn* (Gibb Mem.), p. 470, the word is written *Arkāoun*.
[2] *Synod. Orient.*, pp. 619-620.

On the other hand in the precious semi-official list of the Metropolitans of the Nestorian Church beyond the Oxus and the Far East, compiled by ' Amr,[1] and arranged according to the rank of precedence, we have the following important information : the 14th, the Metropolitan of China ; the 15th, the Metropolitan of India ; the 21st, the Metropolitan of Samarḳand ; the 22nd, the Metropolitan of the Turks ; the 25th, the Metropolitan of Khān Baliḳ and Fāliḳ ; the 26th, the Metropolitan of Tangut ; and the 27th, the Metropolitan of Kashgar and Nuākith.

The strength of the Nestorian Church beyond the Oxus may be gauged from the fact that 'Amr expressly states that each one of the above Metropolitans had either twelve or six Suffragan Bishops under his jurisdiction.

The list of the Nestorian Archbishoprics written by Elijah, Metropolitan of Damascus,[2] is very incomplete, and mentions only Samarḳand (as Kand). Owing to his remoteness from the theatre of events, this Metropolitan knew probably very little of the exact condition of his Church beyond Persia proper.

The principal cities of Central Asia and the Far East, which were the seats of Metropolitans and might have had according to 'Amr from six to twelve Bishops under them were: Samarḳand, Kashgar, Khaṭai, Tangut, and Khān Bāliḳ. We will give below all the references to these Archbishoprics in Syriac and Christian Arabic literature.

SAMARḲAND was the principal town of the ancient province of Sogdiana, situated on the river Soghd, about one hundred and fifty miles east of Bukhara. According to 'Abdīshō' (*Canonical Synods*, cap. xv.) the city was promoted to an Archbishopric by the Patriarch Ṣlība-Zkha (A.D. 712-728), and according to some other authorities it was chosen for that honour by the Patriarch Aḥai (A.D. 410-415), or Shīla (A.D. 505-523),[3] but we believe that these two last dates are somewhat too early. In the quotations which we gave above from the letters of the Patriarch Timothy, there is unfortunately no mention of the precise city to which he ordained the " Bishops of the Turks."

Another important province of the part of the world under consideration, which had been elevated to the rank of an Archbishopric,

[1] *De Pat. Nestor. Comm.*, p. 73 (of the translation).
[2] Assemani, *B.O.*, ii. 458-460.
[3] Cf. *ibid.* iii. 346.

is that of TANGUT. This province gave rise to a kingdom, called by the Chinese Hsi Hsia, which ruled over the present province of Kan-su and adjoining country from A.D. 1004 to 1226, when it was finally destroyed by Chingiz Khan (see d'Ohsson's *Histoire des Mongols*, i. 370 *et sq.*). The people who formed its diocese must have included a considerable number of Turks and Mongols. It was bounded by the Sung Empire on the South and East, by the Khitan on the North-East, the Tartars on the North, the Uighur Turks on the West, and the Tibetans on the South-West. The number of Christians found in the city itself was certainly considerable, and even in the thirteenth century the two monks referred to above—Ṣauma and Marcus—testify to their religious zeal: "They went from there to the town of Tangut. When the inhabitants of the city heard that Fathers Ṣauma and Marcus came there on their way to Jerusalem, they went with diligence to meet them, men and women, young men and children, because the faith of the Tangutians was very staunch and their heart pure."[1] We meet now and then in Syriac literature with the names of its Metropolitans; see, for instance, 'Amr,[2] who among the Bishops who consecrated Yahb-Alāha III. mentions Ishō'-Sabran "Metropolitan of Tangut."[3] In this connection we will refer to the Patriarch Timothy's sentence quoted above concerning the ordination of a Bishop for Tibet, because it is highly probable that the seat of such a Bishop was Tangut, the elevation of which to an Archbishopric will then date back to the end of the eighth Christian century, or about A.D. 790.[4] The Si-ngan-fu of the Nestorian monument in China may have been under the ecclesiastical jurisdiction of Tangut.

A third important city which was the seat of a Nestorian Metropolitan was KASHGAR, the well-known town of Eastern Turkestan, and historically the most important centre of the actual province of Sinkiang. It was almost completely destroyed in the thirteenth century on account of famine and wars, and when the monks Ṣauma and Marcus reached it on their journey to Jerusalem, they found no in-

[1] *Histoire de Yahb-Alāha*, pp. 17-18.

[2] *De Pat. Nest. Comm.* p. 72.

[3] About Tangut in the Lower Middle Ages see Rashīd's *Jāmi' at-Tawarīkh* (Gibb Mem.), pp. 597-599.

[4] About its exact site, see further Bonin, *Journal Asiatique*, 1900, p. 585.

habitants in it at all.[1] But we know that some forty years earlier, or in about 1180, the Patriarch Elijah III. (1176-1190) nominated two Metropolitans for it: a Bishop named John, and after his death another one named Sabrīsho'.[2]

In 845 an edict of the Emperor of China ordered all monks, whether Buddhist or Christian, to become laymen.[3] Christianity, however, did not seem to have been much affected by it, because in an early and important statement the contemporary Patriarch Theodose (852-858) still mentions the Archbishops of Samarḳand, India, and China.[4]

Syriac literature does not clearly indicate the precise time in which a Nestorian Metropolitan was first established in China. We can, however, state with confidence that such an event took place at a relatively early period. The Patriarch Timothy writes about 790 in his book of Epistles,[5] that the Metropolitan of China had died; and Thomas of Marga in the passage quoted above gives us the name of David, the Metropolitan of China, in about 787. All this suggests that China was much earlier than the eighth century the seat of a Metropolitan. We should probably not be far below the boundaries of truth if we were to assume that the Nestorian Church had a Metropolitan in China not later than the seventh century, or about A.D. 670. Prof. Saeki[6] puts forward the plausible hypothesis that the above David was ordained by the Patriarch Timothy as Metropolitan of China in succession to Ching-Ching Adam of the famous Nestorian Monument of Si-ngan-fu. The information furnished by this famous monument erected in 779 (on this date see below pp. 331-333), leads to the same conclusion.

We are in a position to advance a step further in the direction of the introduction of Christianity in China. The document which we are editing and translating in the present study after enumerating the name of four Turkish Christian kings adds that all of them are known by the collective and generic name of *Tatar*, and their country

[1] *Vie de Yahb-Alaha, ibid.* p. 19.
[2] 'Amr, *De Patriar. Nestor. Commentaria*, p. 64 of the translation.
[3] Saeki, *The Nestorian Monument*, p. 47.
[4] Assemani, iv. 439.
[5] *Timothei Epistolæ*, p. 109 (in *C.S.C.O.*).
[6] *The Nestorian Monument in China*, p. 187.

is called Sericon (with a *c* or a *k*). We may state with confidence that the author of the document, whoever he was, was dealing with Mongolia and North China. The well-known name *Tatar* should leave absolutely no doubt in our mind on the subject. Further :—

1. The geographical work of Ptolemy was known to the Syrians.[1] Their books on Geography, Astronomy, and Astrology, testify to this fact ; and it is even probable that parts of the work of the famous Greek geographer were translated by Sergius of Resh'aina who died in 536.[2]

2. Now Ptolemy's geographical work contains a special chapter devoted to *Serice* or *Serike* (book vi. ch. 16). It is bounded according to him on the West by Scythia beyond Imaus, on the North by the Terra Incognita, on the East by the eastern Terra Incognita, and on the South by that part of India that lies beyond the Ganges, and then by the Sinae. In a footnote to Ptolemy's text as cited in *Cathay*[3] the editors add a note to the effect that there is no question that the *Serice* described here is mainly the basin of Chinese Turkestan. (*Ibid.* i. 20 *sq.*) See in this connection the Syriac geographical fragment entitled *Description of the Earth* (purporting to emanate from Ptolemy, king of Egypt !) as printed in *C.S.C.O.*[4] On p. 211 it is maintained that the country of *Seriḳus* is situated East of Scythia and counts no less than sixteen towns. Cf. also *ibid.* (p. 213) the people called *Seriko* and counted side by side with the Scythians.

3. It is highly probable that the Syriac author of the present document applied to North China and Mongolia the name previously assigned to them by Ptolemy whom he was reading either in Greek or in a Syriac translation, because till about the middle of the ninth century Greek constituted an integral part of the curriculum of all the important East and West Syrian schools. All this seems to point to the antiquity of the Syriac document which might thus have been

[1] See, for instance, Syr. MS. No. 44 of the John Rylands Library, and also the geographical section of Barhebraeus's work entitled *Mnārath Ḳudhshé*, etc.

[2] Severius Sabokht who died in 666 may also have had something to do with this translation.

[3] Edit. Yule-Cordier, i. 194.

[4] Third series, vol. vi. pp. 202-213. The work passes under the name of Zacharias Rhetor of the end of the sixth century.

written before all the Medieval and pre-Medieval writers who use in their books the names *Mongolia* or *Khatai* (Cathay). The oldest mention in Syriac literature of China in the form of *Ṣīn*, *Baith Ṣināyé*, or *Ṣinistān* dates, if I mistake not, from the eighth century, and the documents containing these appellations have already been or will presently be quoted. They are the Nestorian monument in China, the letters of Timothy the Patriarch, and the history of Thomas of Marga. The most ancient Syrian writer who mentions China is Bardaiṣan [1] who calls the country *Sher* "Seres" and its inhabitants *Sherāyé* "Sereans." From this vocable is derived the Syriac word *Sherāya* "silk," exactly like the Latin *Sericum* from "Seres."

We must also allude to the fact that the designation of Turkestan and China by the Greek *Serice* (from Seres) is used by some other West Syrian writers, although apparently unknown to Nestorian authors. A rather early Monophysite work [2] calls the Chinese *Seriḳāye*, but the clearest passage in this connection is undoubtedly that of Jacob of Edessa [3] who writes: "All these Empires had risen in this time in the countries of Great Asia, not counting those of the countries of India, nor those of the North, in the countries of Seriḳi, which is called Tasishnisṭan" (vowels uncertain). This sentence is copied verbatim in Michael the Syrian's great history.[4]

The intercourse between China and Mesopotamia has always been constant and active. A king wishing to intimidate a Christian Bishop would threaten to banish him to China,[5] because ships sailing from the Persian Gulf to China and *vice versâ* were an almost daily occurrence.[6]

We do not believe that the Sericon of the geography of the document has anything to do with *Sar-i-kol* or *Sarkol*, the mountainous district of the Chinese Pamirs of which many travellers have spoken at some length. The present capital of the district is Tashkurghan, separated by about fifteen miles from the grazing

[1] *Book of the Laws* (in *Pat. Syr.*) ii. p. 583. See also the so-called "Hymn of the Soul" in the Acts of Thomas: Bedjan's *Acta Martyrum et Sanctorum*, iii. 113.

[2] In Lagarde's *Analecta Syriaca*, pp. 206-207.

[3] *Chronica Minora* (*C.S.C.O.*), p. 283.

[4] i. 120 (edit. Chabot).

[5] *Michael the Syrian* (*ibid.*), ii. 528.

[6] *Ibid.* iii. 61, 84, and many other writers.

grounds of Tagharma, on the main road to Kashgar. The district is in our days inhabited by a considerable number of Aryan population from Western Asia. See A. Stein's *Ruins of Desert Cathay*, i. 89 *seqq.*, and Ella and P. Syke's *Through Deserts and Oases of Central Asia*, pp. 148-174.

In about 1063 the Patriarch Sabrīsho 'III., sent Bishop George to Sijistan and from there to the fourth Nestorian Archbishopric of the Far East: KHATAI, in North China.[1]

It is in place here to remark that the monk Marcus, one of the heroes of the above embassy of the Mongol Emperor Arghūn, had been himself ordained Metropolitan of this Khatai and of Ōng (Hwang ?) by the Patriarch Dinḥa in 1280;[2] this Archbishopric comprised at this period a good belt of Northern China and Manchuria, and seems also to have included some of those Eastern Turks and Mongols better known under the name of Ḳara Khitai.[3] The name is identical with Khata, or Cathay, as North China, or even all China, is designated in some languages.[4] From Syriac sources alone we are not able to locate and name with precision the city which was the seat of this North-China Archbishopric; and, if all signs do not mislead us, we do not believe that there was a Metropolitan of Khatai before the eleventh Christian century. Friar William of Rubruck (*in op. sup. laud.*, p. 244) mentions a Bishop of Cathay in A.D. 1254. More than three centuries previous to this time, Khatai seems to have been a collective name of several Mongolian and Eastern Turkish tribes who inhabited Eastern Manchuria, and who for some two hundred years held China under their sway. In Barhebraeus's *Chron. Syr.* (p. 481, etc.), in Juwaini's *Jahān Gushā* (Gibb Mem., i. 15, etc.), and in Rashīd ad-Dīn's *Jāmi' at-Tawārīkh* (*ibid.* p. 328, etc.) Khatai roughly corresponds with North China. For the delimitation of Ḳara Khitai see Rashīd's *Jāmi'* (*ibid.* p. 397).

Another Bishopric of China, the name of which is mentioned in Syriac literature, is that of the town of Kamul which sent its Bishop John in 1266 to the consecration of the Patriarch Dinḥa.[5] It is the

[1] Mari, *Book of the Tower*, p. 110 of the translation.
[2] *Vie de Yahb-Alāha*, *ibid.* pp. 28-29.
[3] *Vie de Yahb-Alāha*, *ibid.* pp. 29.
[4] Cf. W. Yule-Cordier, *Marco Polo*, *ibid.* i., p. 11, and especially A. Stein, *ibid.*, in *Notes and Addenda*, by H. Cordier, 1920, pp. 53-54.
[5] 'Amr, *ibid.* p. 70.

town called in Mongol Khamil, and in Chinese Hami. See about it Yule-Cordier, *Marco-Polo*, *ibid.* i. 211.

We will here recall the fact that Yahb-Alāha III., the Nestorian Patriarch to whose interesting life we have often referred, was a Chinese born and brought up in Kaushang,[1] situated in Southern Shanhsi, and that his friend and life companion, Ṣauma, was a native of Khān Bālik̩, supposed to be the Peking of our days. 'Amr,[2] however, says that the Patriarch was born in the Khatai which we have discussed above.

A fifth Archbishopric, mentioned by 'Amr in his list, is that of KHĀN BĀLIK̩ and Fālik̩. Sachau[3] believes that Khān Bālik̩ stands for Jān Bālik̩, (a simple change of a dot in the Arabic characters), which has been identified by Bonin[4] with Urumtsi, a town on the great north road from China to Kuldja, and the administrative capital of the actual province of Sinkiang; it is also known under the name of Bish-Bālik. On the other hand, Sachau restores Al-Fālik̩ to Al-Bālik̩ (= Ili-Balik̩) which is to be identified with Almalik of Bonin (*ibid.*), and of Marquart in his *Osteurop. und. Ostas. Streifz.*, p. 498. See about it Rashīd's *Jāmi'* (*ibid.* p. 470).

The Bishopric of Nuākith (= Nawākāth) mentioned by 'Amr in the list which we have quoted above, is that which is referred to by two Arab Geographers, Ibn Khurdadbih and Ḳudāmah[5] as situated in Turkestan, and De Goeje has written its itinerary in parasangs from the town of Tarāz; this itinerary is also found in W. Barthold's monograph *Zur Gesch. des Christentums in Mittel-Asien.*[6] See Marquart's *Eranshahr*, p. 82.

The Nestorian monument of China erected in 779 (on this date see below, pp. 331-333) contains the name of a Bishop John, but unfortunately the town of which he was the Bishop is not mentioned. Further, Friar William of Rubruck,[7] mentions a Nestorian episcopal see in the city of Segin, which is generally identified with Hsi-an-fu, the great centre of Christianity in China in the eighth and ninth

[1] *Vie*, p. 9.
[2] *De Pat. Nestor. Comm.*, p. 71.
[3] *Ausbreitung*, p. 22. [4] *Jour. Asiatique*, 1900, 587.
[5] *Bibliotheca Geograph. Arab.* (edit. De Goeje), vi. 28, 29, 205, 206.
[6] Transl. of R. Stübe, pp. 33 and 34.
[7] *In op. suprà. laud.*, p. 157.

centuries. It is believed that in the thirteenth century the city did not bear the name of Hsi-an-fu, but was called by its older name *Chang-an*, from which William of Rubruck's *Segin*. Objection has been taken to the existence of a Bishopric in this town on the ground that if there was a Bishop in it the above embassy of Mar Yahb-Alaha and Rabban Ṣauma would have visited it on the journey from Kaushang in Southern Shan-hsi to Western Asia. Of all arguments this is one of the flimsiest. Were not the two monks going on pilgrimage to Jerusalem free to follow the route that best suited their plans? Or are we allowed to hold as non-existent any Bishop who does not happen to be mentioned in their narrative?

The activities of the Nestorian Church extended also to the years following this memorable period. Barhebraeus registers the following event under the year 1590 of the Seleucids (A.D. 1279): "In this year a certain Simeon whose surname was *son of Kālij* was Bishop of Ṭūs, a town of Khurāsan. The Catholicos Dinḥa ordained him Metropolitan of the Chinese, but before proceeding to China he began to show recalcitrance towards the Catholicos, who summoned him to the town of Ashnu (Ushnaj) in Adhurbaijan, where he was residing.[1]

In the document called "the History of the Indians"[2] we are informed that the Nestorian Patriarch Elijah V. ordained in A.D. 1503 the following Archbishops: Yahb Alāha, Dinḥa and Jacob and sent them to India, China, and Dabag (= Java).

3. Remaining Traces and Monuments.

Here also we will confine ourselves exclusively to Syriac sources, which we will analyse as follows:—

A.

Monument of Si-ngan-fu.

We could do no better than begin our section with that most famous monument of Si-ngan-fu, the text of which has been edited, translated, and commented upon by many critics since it was first dug out near the district town of Chou-Chih in March, 1625. To our knowledge the most recent and comprehensive (although somewhat

[1] *Chron. Eccles.*, iii. 449. [2] Assem., *B.O.*, iii. 591 *sq.*

popular) work on the subject is that of Professor Saeki entitled *The Nestorian Monument in China* (S.P.C.K. 1916). On the Syriac part of the monument we will venture to make the following observations.

(*a*)

(P. 265, ll. 5, 14.)[1] Many pages have been written by eminent scholars on the subject of the date of the erection of the monument, which is 1092 of the Greeks, as compared with the death of the Patriarch Ḥnānīshō', in whose time the monument was erected. We believe that we are able to remove all chronological difficulties in this connection in the following manner :—

It is a well-known fact among Syriac scholars that the computation of the years of the Seleucids varied in Syrian Churches between 309-313 B.C., and after careful investigations in the works of all Syrian chronologists and historians I have come to the conclusion that it is very unsafe to fix always on 311 as the year to be subtracted from a given Seleucid date in order to obtain the right Christian year. Every case should be taken on its own merits. The Seleucid year 1092 of the monument may, therefore, correspond with any Christian year within 779-783. Now 'Amr[2] followed by Assemani, and by many historians after him, gives the year of the death of the Patriarch Ḥnānīshō' in the Seleucid computation as 1089, but that the dates furnished by the celebrated Christian Arab writer are not always reliable, is proved by the fact that all the elements of the chronological computation of the Festival of Easter, which enter into the cycle of his Seleucid years, are hopelessly wrong. Happily, however, the chronologist Elijah of Nisibin, gives us the year of the Hijrah, and takes us out of the labyrinth of the uncertainties of the year of the Greeks. According to him,[3] Ḥnānīshō' was elected in A.H. 159, and died after a Patriarchate of four years ; his death, therefore, should have occurred in A.H. 163, in which Timothy succeeds him (Elijah, *ibid.* p. 184). A.H. 159 begins on 31st October, 775, and A.H. 163 begins on 17th September, 779. Māri[4] gives the year A.H. 162 for the election of Timothy ; but I believe that he has fallen into a slight chronological

[1] The references are to Saeki's work.

[2] *De Pat. Nestor. Comm.*, p. 37.

[3] *Opus Chronologicum* in *C.S.C.O.*, vol. vii. of the 3rd series, p. 183.

[4] *De Pat. Nestor. Comm.*, p. 63.

error that can easily be explained by the fact that this A.H. 162 begins on the 28th September, i.e. only two days before the beginning of the next year in the Nestorian Ecclesiastical Calendar in which the year began at the sunset of the 30th September or on the eve of 1st October.

The information registered by ʿAmr (*ibid.*) to the effect that the Patriarchate remained vacant for more than a year after the death of Ḥnānishōʿ seems to be unwarranted; indeed all the historians, Barhebraeus,[1] Māri,[2] and Elijah,[3] etc., are of opinion that Timothy was nominated (although somewhat surreptitiously) Patriarch within the limits of the normal delay that accompanied Patriarchal elections in the East, i.e. within the interval of, say, two to four months; further, all the historians agree also that the Patriarchate of Ḥnānīshōʿ lasted four years.

The problem of the precise year of the death of Ḥnānīshōʿ having been elucidated, we will proceed to examine the difficulty of the exact computation of the years of the Seleucids in the eighth Christian century, as compared with the years of the Hijrah. We are happily in a position to solve this difficulty in a safe way through an absolutely unimpeachable source. The Syriac manuscript No. 4 of the John Rylands Library, which contains Biblical and liturgical matter, is copied by a Chinese facsimilist from a Nestorian MS. preserved in Peking. It was either originally written in that city or more probably brought there from the Middle East by one of those very Nestorian missionaries mentioned in the Nestorian monument, because it is dated only twenty-eight years before the erection of the monument (see below, pp. 336-337). The colophon of the MS. is fortunately dated both in the year of the Greeks and in that of the Hijrah. The Greek year which is given in it is written in words and not in figures, and is 1064, and it is said therein to correspond with the year of the Hijrah 134, which is also written in words and not in figures. This proves without any doubt that in the eighth century the Nestorians of Mesopotamia and the Nestorian Missionaries of China counted the era of the Seleucids as 313 B.C. and not 310 or 311, or even 312, because it is only by subtracting 313 from the Seleucid year 1064 that we get A.H. 134. This timely discovery makes the Seleucid year 1092 written on the

[1] *Chron. Eccles.*, ii. 166. [2] *De Patriar.*, p. 63. [3] *Ibid.*

Nestorian monument to correspond with A.D. 779, i.e. the very year of the death of the Patriarch Ḥnānīshō'. The year, therefore, of the erection of the Nestorian monument in Si-ngan-fu is 779, and not 781 as hitherto believed, and there is no discrepancy whatever in the date of the monument as compared with that of the death of the Patriarch Ḥnānīshō'.

(*b*)

(Page 267, line 1.) The first line reads "Yoḥannis, deacon, and *Yadha.*" The last word has been translated by "and the secretary." There is no such a Syriac word in existence, and we believe this translation to be inadmissible; *Yadha* is a shortening of the word *Iḥīdhāya* "monk," which is so often used in the preceding lines. The scribe resorted to abbreviations in this line in order to leave space for the Chinese characters that follow the Syriac ones. The above line should, therefore, be translated by "Yoḥannis (John) deacon and monk."

(*c*)

(Page 265, lines 17-18.) The inscription mentions the name of the priest Yazdbōzid chor-episcopos of Kumdan, son of the priest Miles from Balkh, town of Taḥuristan. The use by a Syrian writer of the Persian termination *Sitān* at the end of a proper name indicates that he was a native of, or brought up or living in, a country stretching from about Central Persia of our days eastwards, and not westwards. To express "Taḥuristan" a Syrian born in the Western side of Central Persia would have used the expression "Beith Taḥūrāye." There is not much doubt in my mind that the majority if not all of the Syriac names appearing in the monument belonged to Christian missionaries who were Persian by birth; indeed the bulk of the Nestorian Church and its most virile element have always been men of what we would call to-day Persian nationality.

B.

GRAVESTONES.

It was in 1885 that some Russian explorers first came into contact with two Nestorian cemeteries of the thirteenth and fourteenth centuries in the Russian province of Semiryechensk in South Siberia, or

Russian Turkestan, near the towns of Pishpek and Tokmak. So far as I can ascertain, more than six hundred and thirty gravestones bearing Syriac inscriptions have since that year been either photographed or brought into the important Museums of Europe, chiefly into Russia. In 1886, 1888 and 1896, Prof. D. A. Chwolson undertook the work of their decipherment in three successive publications presented to the *Académie des Sciences de Saint Pétersbourg*. These worthy publications have formed the basis of many subsequent monographs, the most valuable and detailed of which are those of another Russian scholar Kokowzoff. The most ancient gravestone so far discovered is not earlier than about the middle of the ninth century, and the latest may be ascribed to about the middle of the fourteenth century. Cf. *Journal Asiatique* (9th series), 1896, viii. p. 428, and Nöldeke in *Z.D.M.G.* xliv. 520-528.

Gravestones erected in the form of a cross have also been discovered in Manchuria (*Journal Asiatique*, *ibid.* pp. 428-429) and Nayan, King of that country, was a Christian and had inscribed the Sign of the Cross on his banners.

The dates used in the above inscriptions are those of the Seleucid era, which has been in constant use in the Nestorian Church, and those of the Turco-Mongolian cycle of 12 years which bore the names of rat, ox, tiger, rabbit, dragon, snake, horse, sheep, monkey, hen, dog, and pig.

The Christian community of that almost lost corner of the earth must have been fairly considerable, because among the about three hundred gravestones of men, published by Chwolson, there are nine archdeacons, eight doctors of ecclesiastical jurisprudence and of Biblical interpretation, twenty-two visitors, three commentators, forty-six scholastics, two preachers and an imposing number of priests.

The names borne by the members of this Christian community are highly interesting for the Turkish onomastical science; but here and there one picks up names of a decidedly Greek origin, quite distinguished from those names that are sanctioned in the Old and New Testaments; ex. gr. Julia. A unique feature in their case is the use of the name *Kushṭanz*, which Chwolson identifies with *Constance*, as a second member of a formative compound; so we meet with names of Mary Kushtanz, Rebecca Kushtanz, Ṣalība Kushtanz, etc. Another interesting feature of the proper names is that Syriac abstract and concrete nouns are pressed into use, apparently on account of the paucity of Christian names in that part of the world ; so we find Shlāma (Peace), Ṭaibūtha (Grace), Shilya (Quiet), Shlīḥa (Apostle or the Naked One), Ṣimḥa (Ray), Pisḥa (Passover). Some of the inhabitants were also related to the country from which either they or their fathers had hailed ; so a woman is called " Terim[1] the Chinese," a priest figures as " Banūs, the Uighurian " and a layman as " Sāzīk the Indian " ; another is " Ḳiamta of Kashgar," and yet another " Taṭṭa, the Mongol " ; ner a periodeuta " Shāh-Maliḳ " is a son of a George of Ṭūs " ; and six persons are related to the city of Al-Malig. All these names imply a constant intercourse between the different Christian peoples of Central Asia and the Far East ; without such an intercourse we are not able to explain satisfactorily the fact that we have side by side in a single cemetery people from China, India, East and West Turkestan, Mongolia, Manchuria, Siberia, and Persia.

To give our readers an idea of these important gravestones we shall give the translation of five of them :—

(Chwolson, vol. iii. 18, No. 66) : " In the year one thousand six hundred and twenty-three, which is the year of the pig. This is the grave of the Priest Peter, the venerable old man."

(Chwolson, vol. i. 14, and vol. ii. 55) : " In the year one thousand six hundred and twenty-seven, which is the year of the dragon, in Turkish " Lowū ". This is the grave of Shlīḥa, the celebrated commentator and teacher, who illuminated all the monasteries with light ; son of Peter the august commentator of Wisdom. His voice rang as high as the sound of a trumpet. May our Lord mix his pure soul with the just men and the Fathers. May he participate in all (heavenly) joys."

(Chwolson, vol. iii. 16, No. 52) : " In the year 1616, which is that of the Turkish snake. This is the grave of Sabrīshō', the archdeacon, the blessed old man, and the perfect priest. He worked much in the interests of the church."

(Chwolson, vol. iii. 14, No. 47) : " In the year 1613. This is the grave of the priest Isaac, the blessed old man. He worked much in the interests of the town."

[1] This name Terim frequently figures in the inscriptions, and is doubtless formed from the well known river Tarim, in Chinese Turkestan.

(Chwolson, vol. iii. 16, 57): "In the year one thousand six hundred and eighteen, which is the year of the sheep. This is the grave of Jeremiah, the believer."

C.

Liturgical MSS.

(*a*)

In 1905 the German explorer Von Le Coq discovered in Chinese Turkestan some leaves containing portions of a Nestorian Breviary and Liturgy. They have been edited and translated by Sachau in *Sitzung. d. Kön. Preus. Akad. d. Wissen.*, 1905, pp. 964-973.

Sachau has identified most of the passages from the "Gazza" and the "Ḥudhra" of the Nestorians, and has rightly ascribed the script used in these interesting finds to the tenth or ninth century. The latter date is probably nearer to the mark than the former. The other passages which Sachau seems to have been unable to identify are also found in many MSS. of the service-books of the Church, and some may even be verified in the printed text published by Bedjan under the title of *Breviarium Chaldaicum* (Paris, 1886).

(*b*)

On pp. 973-978 Sachau has also published another find of Le Coq's in Chinese Turkestan, in the form of a leaf written in Syriac characters and exhibiting a Christian treatise composed in one of the middle Persian dialects of Central Asia, called Soghdian.

Far more important than the above piece are the Soghdian fragments also in Syriac characters published by F. W. K. Müller in the *Abhandlungen* of which we shall speak below. On pp. 87-88 of this publication we read in Syriac characters and in the Syriac language the *Credo* as used in the official books of the Nestorian Church, where it is attributed to the Fathers of the Council of Nicæa.

(*c*)

As important as the above finds is the Syr. MS. No. 4 of the John Rylands Library. It is a facsimile on Chinese paper, and made by a Chinese hand, before 1727—of an ancient Syriac Biblical and liturgical volume which in 1727 was still in possession of a Chinese mandarin of Peking.

The original MS. upon which the Chinese facsimilist was working is apparently still preserved in China. It is dated as stated above 1064 of the Greeks, and 134 of the Hijrah, and written in the time of Cyprian, Metropolitan of Nisibin. The fact that a Metropolitan of Nisibin is mentioned in the colophon seems to suggest that at least one of the missionaries who brought the MS. with them to China was living under the ecclesiastical jurisdiction of that famous Metropolis of the East Syrian Church. For further details of this MS. see our *Brief Descriptive Catalogue of the Syriac MSS. in the John Rylands Library*. It is neither a complete Bible, nor a complete liturgical book, nor a complete service-book, but it contains the most necessary parts of each ; just the kind of vade-mecum of Bible, liturgy, and breviary which a missionary would carry about with him from place to place, and through which he might satisfy all his devotional requirements with ease.

(*d*)

In the library of the Chaldean (Nestorian Uniate) Bishopric of Diarbekr there is a Syriac Lectionary of the Gospels written in letters of gold upon a blue background. The colophon of this MS., which has been published by Pognon,[1] informs us that it was written in 1609 of the Greeks (1298 A.D.), for the queen Arangul, the sister of Georges, king of the Christian Turks called Ganaṭu-Uriyang. Blochet,[2] who has discussed this colophon, arrives at the only possible conclusion that the name represents the powerful Turkish agglomeration of tribes called Uriyan-gaḳit, who must thus have been undoubtedly Christian in 1298.[3]

The above king is probably the King Georges of Marco Polo and John of Monte Corvino. He was killed in Mongolia in 1298 (the very year of the transcription of the Lectionary) leaving an infant child baptised by Monte Corvino. See Pelliot, *T'oung Pao*, 1914, p. 632 *sq*. and *Cathay*, 1916, iii. 15 (edit. Yule-Cordier).

We will here refer also to another Nestorian Lectionary of the Gospels described by Blochet in his Persian catalogue of the Paris MSS. and written apparently in Samarḳand in A.D. 1374.

[1] *Inscriptions Sémitiques*, p. 137.
[2] *Introduction à l'Histoire des Mongols*, p. 181.
[3] Cf. Rashīd's *Jāmiʿ at-Tawārīkh* (Gibb Mem.), p. 385, etc.

Finally we should not overlook the fact that in the Middle Ages there were so many Christian Turks and Mongols in Central Asia, Persia, and Mesopotamia, that Nestorian hymn-writers were obliged to compose some hymns for their exclusive benefit in what they called Mongolian. So Khāmis, the famous Nestorian hymn-writer, composed the *Soghītha* beginning with "The Son of Mary is born to us" in alternate strophes, one in Syriac and the other in Mongolian (= Eastern Turkish). This hymn which is also mentioned below is found in some other MSS., ascribed to Khāmis; see, for instance, vol. ii., p. 693, of Wright's & Cook's *Catalogue of the Syriac MSS. of Cambridge.*

(*e*)

Among the discoveries made near Turfan in Chinese Turkestan, are some fragments of complete leaves or parts of leaves of a Lectionary of the Gospels as used in the Nestorian Community of that part of the world. The indications of the lessons to be recited in Churches are generally in complete agreement with those of the official Nestorian Christianity of Mesopotamia and Persia. The date of the leaves cannot be later than the tenth century. They are mostly written in Syriac characters, but in the Soghdian dialect of Middle Persian interspersed with complete sentences in the Syriac language. They have been edited and translated by F. W. K. Müller in the above *Abhandlungen d. Preus. Akad. d. Wissen.* (1912, 1-111). They contain sixteen quotations from Matthew, nineteen from Luke, fifteen from John, three from 1 Corinthians, and one from Galatians, and all are in almost complete agreement with the sacred text used by the Nestorian Church. The indications of the Soghdian Lectionary have been compared with those furnished by the official Church Books of the Nestorians by Burkitt in his interesting little book, *The Religion of the Manichees,* 1925, pp. 121-123.

D.

Manichæan Writings.

It is not our intention here to mention all the Manichæan documents discovered in the last few years in Central Asia by the Russian, German, French, and British scientific missions. They are admirably enumerated and classified in that instructive book of P. Alfaric, entitled "Les Ecritures Manichéennes" (vol. i. 1918, *Vue Générale,* and vol. ii., 1919, *Étude Analytique*). The only authoritative book on the subject after Alfaric's is Le Coq's *Die Buddhistische Spät. in Mittelasien*, 1923. We will refer, however, to those of them which are written in Syriac characters, and which contain decidedly Christian matter which could not have emanated except from Nestorians living side by side with the Manichæans of those countries. Some of these have already been mentioned above. The remaining ones may be classified as follows:—

(*a*)

In 1904 Mr. C. Salemann translated in the Proceedings of the Imperial Academy of Sciences of Saint Petersburg a leaf discovered near Turfan written both in Chinese and in Syriac characters of about the ninth century. The Syriac fragment is important because it refers to some other works of the Manichæans which are lost in our days.

(*b*)

The most important publication in the field of knowledge with which we are dealing is undoubtedly F. W. K. Müller's work entitled "Handschriften-Reste in Estrangelo-Schrift aus Turfân" in the *Abhandlungen* of the Prussian Academy of 1904, pp. 1-117, the first part of which was published eight years later in the same series, and is referred to above under C (*e*).

Specially illuminating is the story of the Passion and Crucifixion of Jesus as narrated in the fragments edited on pp. 34-37, in which the proper names found in the Gospels are given in their Syriac form. Attention should also be drawn to the Manichæan *Sanctus* of pp. 70-73 where the word for "holy" is the Syriac *Ḳdhōsh* contracted from *Ḳudhsha*,[1] On p. 94 Jesus is spoken of under the Syriac formula of "Bar Maryam" *the Son of Mary*. This formula is repeated in every verse of the above *Sōghītha* of Dominical Festivals in the Nestorian liturgical books, beginning "the Son of Mary is born to us."[2]

[1] In a document on p. 87 the word *Turan* is used of the Turks. If the date assigned to these documents is correct the Soghdian fragment would contain one of the oldest mentions so far made of the Turks under the appellation *Turanians*.

[2] In Syr. MS. marked Mingana 129, recently brought from the East, this *Sōghītha* is attributed also to Khāmis, the well-known Nestorian hymn-writer.

We cannot here refrain from quoting some passages referring to the Passion and Crucifixion of Jesus. The fragment that contains them is unfortunately very defective ; we will indicate its lacunæ by means of three dots. Its title is "An extract on the Crucifixion" and its text begins with the words "if in truth He is the Son of God," and continues :—[1]

"And Pilate answered 'I am innocent of the blood of this Son of God.' Then the officers and soldiers received from Pilate the following order : 'Keep this commandment secret. . . .' He shows that on a Sunday at the first crow of the cock, Maryam, Shalom and (Arsāniyah) came with other women and brought perfumes of nard. Nearing the grave they . . . see the splendour. . . . As did Maryam, Shalom and Arsaniyah (sic) when the angels said to them, 'Seek not the living among the dead.' Think of the words of Jesus addressed to you in Galilee, 'they will deliver Me and crucify Me, and on the third day I shall rise from the dead.' Go to Galilee and communicate this news to Simon and the others."

Müller (*ibid.* p. 109) believes that this narrative agrees with the apocryphal Gospel of Peter ; this may be true of the first part of it, but certainly not of the second part ; further the Gospel of Peter has never had any influence on the Nestorian Community, and was probably unknown even on the eastern banks of the Tigris. We believe therefore that the above extracts represent a Nestorian Christian composition clumsily quoted in a Manichæan work. What would lend a colour of plausibility to this view is the form and pronunciation of the proper names, which have a clear and distinct Nestorian savour.

Müller[2] has also given us the translation of an interesting and original hymn-book of the Manichees. Some hymns in the collection are decidedly under Christian influence, and "Jesus the Messiah," in Syr. *Ishō' Mshīḥa*, used in them is an expression which could not have been known except through that influence :—

"We wish to celebrate Thee O Jesus, the Messiah. . . . We wish to praise Thee O blessed Spirit. . . . We wish to extoll Thee, O High God. . . . I am the Spirit that lives."

In a fragment discovered in 1905 at Bulayik, north of Turfan,

[1] Müller *Handschriften Rest.*, pp. 34-36.

[2] *Ein doppelblatt aus einem Manich. Hymnenbuch*, in the *Abhandlungen* of the Prussian Academy, 1913, p. 28.

occurs the name *Zawtai* for Zebedee, the father of the Evangelist John. Now the letter B is not softened into "V" and then changed in pronunciation into "W" except among the East Syrians or Nestorians [1] with whom the word under consideration is read as *Zawdai*:—

"The eighteenth oracle—it is a good one. Thus speaks Zawtai [2] the Apostle: "O Son of Man, you resemble the cow that from far lowed to her straying calf. As this young calf heard the voice of his mother and ran quickly to her, and in this way escaped injury, so also yours . . . which from far . . . rapidly with great joy."

"The nineteenth oracle—it is a bad one. Thus speaks Luke the Apostle: "O Son of Man, wash your hand. Do not have any fear before evil. Have pure thoughts. The love that you conceive for God, realise it openly." [3]

E.

Central Asian Alphabets.

We need not dwell here on the well-known fact that the Syriac characters as used by the Nestorians gave rise to many Central Asian and Far Eastern alphabets such as the Mongolian, the Manchu, and the Soghdian. The existing characters of the two former groups of languages are lineal descendants of the original Uighurian forms which were certainly derived from the Nestorian Syriac characters, under the influence of the civilised Christian community of Uighuria.

F.

Miscellanies.

(*a*)

In a private family at Mosul, in North Mesopotamia, I saw an iron cross of a fairly large size with inscriptions in Syriac and in Chinese.

[1] See my Syriac Grammar: *Clef de la Langue Araméenne*, No. 3.

[2] There is no question here of the problematical disciple Zabdai as Alfaric (*ibid.* ii. 180) believes, but, as the name of Luke suggests in the next oracle, Zabdai designates here the Apostle John the Evangelist. The word *Bar* "Son of" has been omitted, as it is often done by the copyists; and the Eastern habit of calling the son by the name of his father or *vice versâ* is too well known to need explanation.

[3] Von Le Coq, *Ein Christliches . . . Manuskriptfragment* in *Sitzungsberichte* of the Prussian Academy, 1909, pp. 1202, 1205-1208. The fragment has unfortunately many lacunæ.

The Syriac words read: *Ṣlība zkha*, "Crux vicit" (the cross has conquered), but I was not able to read the Chinese characters which occupied an even shorter space. The cross may have been imported from China by a Nestorian missionary, or a Christian Chinese warrior in the Mongol army.

(*b*)

There are coins of the Mongolian Il-Khāns, called "coins of the cross," which bear the Christian legend, "In the name of the Father, the Son, and the Holy Ghost, one God." For the dirham coins of the Emperor Abāḳa which have this legend, see *Journal Asiatique*, 1896 (9th series), vii. 514, and for some coins of the Emperor Arghūn, which also bear this Christian legend (see *ibid.* 1896, viii. 333). The respect in which even the non-Christian Mongol Kings, and Khans, held the Nestorians is best illustrated by the fact that they used to take off their headgear and genuflect before their Patriarch (*ibid.* xiii. 1881, the Jan. number).

(*c*)

The influence which the Nestorian Christians exercised on the Turks, even on those among them who were Mohammedans, may be emphasised by the fact that about A.D. 1200 Sulaiman of Bāḳirghān, in the Khānate of Khiva, composed in Turki, or the Eastern Turkish dialect, a poem on the death of the Virgin, the contents of which were inspired by Nestorian writings on the same subject (cf. Congrès des Orientalistes d'Alger, 3rd part, 1907, pp. 28 *sq.*).

(*d*)

Finally, we will mention here the fact that a great Nestorian writer, the author of the *Gannath Bussāmé*, was towards the end of the twelfth century entrusted with the exposition of the Christian doctrine and the interpretation of Church Lectionaries of the Old and New Testaments to the numerous Christian Turks and Mongols inhabitating Persia and Mesopotamia, and he was for that called "The Interpreter of the Turks" *par excellence*.

For further details on Christianity in Central Asia and the Far East in the Middle Ages, from Chinese and Muslim sources, which do not constitute a part of our enquiry, we recommend the following works: W. Barthold's Monograph *Christentums in Mittel Asien*,

1901; Yule-Cordier, *Cathay and the way thither* (Hakluyt Society), vols. i.-iv., 1915-1916; Cordier, *Le Christianisme en Chine et en Asie sous les Mongols*, Leiden, 1918; Pelliot, *Chrétiens d'Asie Centrale* (in T'oung-Pao, 1914).

II.

We give in the following pages the translation of a Syriac document attributed to Akhsnāya, or the famous monophysite Philoxenus, Bishop of Mabbug, who died in Gangra of Paphlagonia in A.D. 523. He is one of the most eminent writers of Syriac, and to theological students he is better known as the author of the Philoxenian Version of the Bible. His life in a more or less accurate form can be found in almost all the books of reference, but the present writer believes that he was the last to discuss in 1920 some aspects of his life and of his Biblical work.[1]

The present document is two-fold. More than half of it deals with the Christian heresies that preceded the author's time. Very briefly he gives their main Christological features and sketches the history of the Councils who condemned them. The second part of the document outlines the introduction of Christianity among the Turks, and possesses by the freshness of its contents an importance which could not be paralleled by anything said in the first part. The Christian heresies mentioned in the first part are those of Sabellius, Paul of Samosata, Arius, Eusebius of Cæsarea, Macedonius, Nestorius, and Eutyches. A larger space is naturally devoted to the last heretic but one and to Theodore of Mopsuestia, and his hatred for both of them knows no bounds; were they not the Nestorians who had driven him out of Garamea, his native country, and applied to him the epithet of the "accursed wolf?"[2] Our modern civilisation has at least done something good: it has in some countries of Europe begun to sweep away that fanatical spirit whereby a man would persecute, or maim, or even kill a human being for his religious beliefs, and think that he was offering a sacrifice to God. The true spirit of Christ was sadly deficient in the fifth and sixth centuries, and this

[1] *A New Document on Philoxenus of Hierapolis*, *Expositor*, 1920, pp. 149-160.

[2] Bābai the Great, quoted in our *Narsai Homiliae et Carmina*, vol. i. p. 6 of the introduction.

deficiency explains the stringency of the style used by many ecclesiastical writers of the time, including Philoxenus.

We give the translation of this part of the document without any comment. Its merits and demerits can be judged by every theologian interested in Church history and in the Christological discussions which—in the centuries where kings were effectively dabbling in religion—rent asunder the coherent body of the Christian community. The author, living far from the scene of events, has fallen into some slight chronological errors, and presented the philosophical aspect of the questions in a light which is somewhat foreign to our upbringing. We write no corrective notes to statements which can easily be verified by any intelligent reader, in order to reserve our space to the second part of the document which is of particular interest for the history of the spread of Christianity beyond the Oxus.

One of the strongest reasons urged by some critics against the authenticity of the first part of the letter which deals with Christian heresies, and which is already known from the British Museum MSS. spoken of below, is the glaring anachronism which in the narrative makes Theodore of Mopsuestia a contemporary and fellow student of Nestorius. The difficulty, however, has been explained by Nau,[1] who, after his publication of a summary of Barṣalībi's work against the Nestorians, was able to show that the Theodore of the present document is a deliberate error on the part of the copyist for Theodoret of Cyrus. To follow up his intentional falsification the scribe had also the audacity of changing Cyrus into Mopsuestia, and in converting in one place the name of the Emperor Theodosius into that of Honorius. That the forefathers of Nestorius were of Persian extraction, as presented in the present Jacobite document, may be gathered from the fact that the Nestorians also are of the same opinion. The lexicographer, Bar 'Ali,[2] expressly states that Atak is the "name of the village of Addaī, grandfather of Nestorius." Where Nestorians and Jacobites agree we may be fairly certain that we are treading on firm ground. Finally, we must also add that the letter to Abū 'Afr is mentioned among the authentic works of Philoxenus by the author of his life which we published in 1920.[3]

[1] *Revue de l'Orient Chrétien*, 1909, p. 424 *sq.*, cf. *ibid.* p. 301 *sq.*

[2] Payne Smith's *Thesaurus Syriacus*, i. 422 (the word *Ḳashshīsha* is here to be understood in the sense of "grandfather," and not that of "presbyter").

[3] *Expositor*, 1920, p. 154.

We need not dwell on the subject of the authenticity of the document. We simply cannot make ourselves believe that it emanates from Philoxenus, at least not from the Philoxenus whom we so well know by almost innumerable works on theological and mystical sciences. The most charitable hypothesis that we may put forward in this connection is that if the precious document is in any way connected with him, he must have written it in his youth, and in this case it would represent the first intellectual élan of an exuberant genius before attaining its full-fledged mental acumen.

The document does not lose much of its value by not having been written by Philoxenus. All the works attributed to a certain Father of the Church may not have been actually written by him, and there are certainly treatises passing under the name of this or that Greek, Latin, or Syriac Father which are as far from having emanated from him as the present document from Philoxenus, but their internal value is in no way impaired by this fact. To add a kind of a nominal value to an anonymous tract, a copyist was in some cases tempted to ascribe it to a well-known author; in some other cases a young and obscure writer, wishing to draw attention to a subject to which he attached special importance, would deliberately use the name of a highly respected and widely known man in order to obtain better reading. It is from the rank of these pious or impious forgers that the list of the apocryphal literature found in the historical archives of almost every religious and political community, has been unduly swollen.

Although apparently not by Philoxenus the document is very ancient; the MS. Add. 14529[1] of the British Museum, ascribed by Wright to the seventh or eighth Christian century, contains that section of it which deals with Nestorius and Eutyches, and as such it has been edited by P. Martin in his *Introductio practica ad studium linguae Arameae*, 1873, and translated by J. Tixeront in *Revue de l'Orient Chrétien*, 1903, 623-630.[2] Short fragments of this very section of the text are also to be seen in Brit. Mus. Add. 17193 and 17134 (pp. 338 and 998 in Wright's Catalogue). The text, however, of the British Museum MS. contains deep variants and many omissions when compared with that which we are translating in the present study. It

[1] Wright's *Catalogue*, ii. 917-918.
[2] Cf. A. Vaschalde, *Three Letters*, 1902, p. 30.

is not our intention to dwell on the explanation of the verbal differences which separate the two recensions.

The document is in form of a letter addressed to Abū 'Afr, military Governor of Ḥīrah. The British Museum MS. calls him Abu Naphīr, and our MS. Abu (gen. Abi) 'Afr. The reading of our MS. has unexpectedly been confirmed by that interesting and important Syriac work dealing with the Christian martyrs of the Yaman, and entitled *Book of the Ḥimyarites*, which has been lately unearthed and so ably edited by the Swedish scholar A. Moberg.[1] The name Abu 'Afr clearly occurs in this work as an Arabic proper name on fol. 24b. In the life of Philoxenus that we published in 1920 the name occurs as Abu Ḥafr.[2] The Muslim tradition,[3] however, calls him *Abu Ya'fur*, and gives his genealogy as b. 'Alḳamah, b. Mālik, b. 'Adī, b. Dhumail, b. Thaur, b. Asas, b. Rubay, b. Numārah, b. Lakhm. According to the Arab historians (*ibid.*) he succeeded Nu'mān b. Aswad in the government of Ḥīrah and reigned three years. The Syriac *Abi 'Afr* of the document can also be read as *Ab Ya'fur* in conformity with Arab sources.

Our present study is based on the Syriac MS. 59 of the John Rylands Library (ff. 99a-107b), which to our knowledge is the only one that contains in full the letter of Philoxenus to Abū 'Afr; it is dated 29th January, 1909, but the deacon Matti, the copyist, assured us verbally, when we met him last year in the East, that he had transcribed it from a vellum MS. found in Ṭur 'Abdīn, which he would ascribe at the latest to the eleventh century. It formerly constituted a part of the writer's collection of Syriac MSS. where it was numbered: Mingana 9.

The section dealing with the Turks to which the main part of our study is devoted evidently emanates from a zealous Jacobite who was eager to show that his Church also, and especially his Patriarchate of Antioch, had some share in the conversion of the Turks, and while the Christian peoples beyond the Oxus swore allegiance to the Nestorian Patriarch of Ctesiphon, and technically belonged to his Nestorian community, they did so *bonâ fide* and by force of circumstances,

[1] *The Book of the Himyarites . . . A hitherto unknown Syriac work*, Leipzig and Lund, 1924.

[2] *Expositor*, 1920, p. 154.

[3] Tabari, *Annales*, 1, 2, 900; Ibn Duraid, p. 266; Ibn al-Athīr, *Kāmil*, i. 154 (edit. Bulāḳ).

ultimately due to the long distance that separated them from the monophysite Patriarch of Antioch. This is of course an *ex-parte* statement which should be received with great caution. There are no grounds whatever for denying the incontrovertible fact that the glory of converting the peoples of Central Asia and of the Far East to the Gospel of Christ, and the merit of implanting among them the Western civilisation, based on the teaching of Jesus of Nazareth, belong entirely to the untiring zeal and the marvellous spiritual activities of the Nestorian Church, which is by far the greatest missionary Church that the world has ever produced. Even we, hard critics and unprejudiced inquirers, who are writing centuries after the events, cannot but marvel at the love of God, of man, and of duty, which animated those unassuming disciples of Christ, true pupils of their Apostles Addai and Thomas, who in utter disregard of all discomforts of the body, and in the teeth of the strong opposition and the terrible vengeance of the wizards of Shamanism and the mobeds of Zoroastrianism, literally explored all the corners of the Eastern globe in order to sow in them the seed of what they firmly believed to be the true religion of God. All glory to them!

There are in the document some proper names which are very difficult to identify. They belong to the Eastern section of the Central Asian peoples. Four of these names are those of the Christian kings whom the author is mentioning:[1] Gawirk, Girk, Ṭasahz, and Langu. The precise country in which they lived was called Sericon; the border town of this country was called Ḳaragūr[am], and the name of its King was Idiḳūt. Five days' journey separated Ḳaragūr[am] from the habitat of the Christian Turks. We have done our best to illustrate the above names in the footnotes from Greek, Syriac, Arabic, Persian, Turkish, and Mongolian sources, but we were not able to identify some of them with any degree of probability in the literatures of these languages. Their exact identification may possibly be effected through Chinese sources, but these we could not cite with authority as we do not know any Chinese at all.

We have also ventured to add some footnotes to illustrate or explain the historical data of the document. From these notes the reader will be able to form an independent judgment on the value to

[1] The vowels of all the names are uncertain.

be attached to the information imparted by the author. Nearly all the historical data furnished by him have, on verification, proved genuine and correct in every important detail, but the confidence with which the document thus inspires us will be strengthened by the knowledge that all the names of kings and towns mentioned in it are found in Chinese sources which we were unfortunately unable to consult at first hand.

This second part of the document which concerns the Christian Turks seems to be only loosely attached to the first part which deals with Christian heresies, and it is possible that it was pieced together with it by an ancient copyist from a totally different MS. Indeed if we join the sentence of p. 360: "a great number of people deviated from the path of truth and became Nestorians, on account of the severity of the persecution," with that of p. 366: "the occasion of this arose at the time when persecution was aflame against the Christians of the countries of the Persians at the hand of the accursed Barṣauli of Nisibin," we will have a somewhat homogeneous and continuous composition, and all the text written between the two phrases will appear as an interpolation. The argument, however, should not be unduly pressed because the same process might with almost equal success be applied to the beginning of the history of Nestorius as compared with the way in which the previous heresies of Sabellius, Paul of Samosata, Arius, and Macedonius are introduced.

Further, the opinion that the text of all the document dealing with the Christian Turks is taken from a completely different MS. seems to be borne out by the following fact. On p. 362 occurs the phrase: "the see of their Bishop is in the pagan town which we have mentioned *above*." Now no Turkish town of any kind is mentioned in the pages that precede this sentence. It seems, therefore, plausible that this part of the document was transcribed by a copyist from another MS. and inserted in the present document purporting to be written by Philoxenus on the Christian heresies that preceded him, because the name of the Turkish town must have been mentioned in the previous part of the text which has been omitted by the copyist.

We must finally state here that this opinion clears up the difficulty arising out of the *mise en scène* of the present state of the document. Indeed, from its text as it stands before us, it would be difficult to understand what induced Philoxenus to apprise a military Governor of

Ḥīrah of the introduction of Christianity among the Turks. What interest had Ḥīrah with the Turks in the fifth Christian century? And why should Philoxenus have spoken of the Turks at all in a letter on Christian heresies?

We have seen in the first half of the document that the copyist in order to cover up, or rather to follow up the error of his confusion of Theodore with Theodoret was compelled to change Cyrus into Mopsuestia, and Theodosius into Honorius. The same process of deliberate falsifications seems to have been adopted in the second part. The work is introduced by the entrance into the scene, on the one hand, of the Jacobite Philoxenus and Abu 'Afr, and on the other of the Nestorian Acacius and Barṣauma. All these are contemporaries and constitute an integral part of the drama. Within the frame assigned to them all the other *dramatis personæ* are more or less loosely introduced, including the Christian Turks.

The scene of the arrival of these Turks is placed in the fifth century, during the Patriarchate of Acacius. This is possible but not probable, because we believe that the document was composed by a Jacobite writer after the Arab invasion. In it occurs the Arabic word *salm* which we consider to be a copyist's error for *sanim* which means "a big humped camel." In it also there is mention of circumcision, which, more probably, refers to Muslims. The Christian Turks, it is said, killed any one they saw circumcised like pagans. The adherents of Christianity could not possibly have been in the fifth century so numerous and powerful in Central Asia as to kill any pagan with whom they happened to meet; further, we have no reason for supposing that circumcision was ever practised by any important section of the pagan Turks and Tartars. The pagans spoken of in the document can in our judgment refer only to Muslims.

The precise year in which the document was written in the time of the Arab Empire will probably never be determined. The date of the MS. is according to Shammas Matti—who knows a great deal about Syriac MSS. and who has copied more of them than any other man living or dead—at the latest about the first half of the eleventh century, say 1040. We must, therefore, fix for the composition of the document on a date within the limits of A.D. 680-1000. This being the case we believe as a matter of opinion that the document was composed about 730-790 by a Jacobite writer living in Baghdad.

The precise, valuable, and on the whole accurate information that he furnishes concerning the Turks and Tartars, their country and their habits, may have been taken orally by him from a Turkish deputation that must have waited upon a Nestorian Patriarch (see above pp. 304 and 306) for the ordination of a Metropolitan to their country.

This opinion is only provisional and will naturally be subject to revision upon the right identification of the proper names mentioned in the document; but apart from its intrinsic plausibility it can also safeguard the view of those scholars who, relying on the date of the British Museum MS., which according to Wright is not later, but rather earlier, than the eighth century, would prefer to regard all the document as one indivisible whole. About the antiquity of the document from the use of the archaic geographical term *Sericon* see pp. 326-327.

The Syrian author of the document had acquired from this supposed Christian Turkish mission or from other sources unknown to us, some knowledge of the history of Turkestan and China, because he has actually placed the scene of his drama at the end of the fifth century and at the beginning of the sixth, i.e. at a time corresponding with A.D. 455 and 513, in which no less than ten diplomatic missions are recorded as passing between Northern China and Persia. See Saeki, *The Nestorian Monument*, pp. 39-47, etc. Hirth, *China and the Roman Orient* (passim), and the very well-known works of Chavannes. On the other hand the eighth century is also conspicuous by such missions; from Hirth's and Chavannes' works we gather that for the first half of this century the following missions took place between Western and Eastern Asia, in 701, 719, 732, and 742.

Against the indications of the MSS. which ascribe the document to Philoxenus we have ventured to argue in favour of the probability of the opinion that it was written after the Arab invasion. On the other hand we must admit that the hypothesis which we have set forth as to the double character of the document is not so well founded and should on no account be considered more than possible, because it is equally plausible that the document as we have it in its complete form in our MS. and in its discontinuous and truncated shape in the British Museum MSS. may have been written in its totality by one author. All this is fairly clear. Somewhat less clear is the precise year or decade in which the document saw the light. Here on grounds both extrinsic and intrinsic we have adhered to the view that its probable date was the eighth century, or more precisely a date between 730 and 790, that is to say the time in which the Nestorian Church seems to have displayed special energy in its foreign missions.

We have already avowed our complete ignorance of Chinese language and literature, but this should not impede us from appealing to at least two of those Chinese scholars who have spoken of the Tartars from exclusively Chinese sources in the hope of corroborating some historical points to which we drew attention above.

On p. 347 we gave the names of the Christian kings mentioned in the document. Among them is one whose name is in consonants TASHZ and another LNGU. In E. H. Parker's *A Thousand Years of the Tartars* (p. 271), we find an account of a Turkish general called Tsz-i who in 756 was assisted by Maryenchö against the rebel Amroshar. The latter, after conducting the war against the Cathayans, as China's representative, in the end rebelled against his imperial master. Parker adds that this "celebrated general Tsz-i" is believed to have been a Nestorian Christian. In Saeki's *The Nestorian Monument in China* (p. 55) he is described as a "believer in the Nestorian religion." He lived A.D. 697-781, just within the chronological limits prescribed by our document.

The above identification seems to be plausible and should, I believe, be considered as probable. For the other Christian kings we find less convincing evidence in Chinese literature. So far as LNGU is concerned were it not for reasons of chronology we might have compared him with Li-Yüan,[1] whose father had married a Nestorian Christian lady of the Duku family. A short time after his death, or in 635, the famous Nestorian missionary Olopen[2] arrived in China. In this time the grandson of the Christian lady, who had become Emperor, issued an edict in favour of Christianity.

For GWRK and GRK, the other two Christian kings mentioned in the document, we may compare Kuang (the interchange between *n*

[1] Parker (*ibid.*), p. 194, and Saeki (*ibid.*), pp. 204-208.

[2] Olopen or Alopen has been conjectured to represent any of the following Syriac words: *Rabban* "our master" (title of a monk), or *Yahb-Alāha*, a proper name meaning "Deo-datus," or *Abraham*. See Saeki, *ibid.* pp. 204-207.

and *r* is fairly common), the son of the Emperor Hsuan-Tsung, who in 755 together with Jacob, the son of the Christian king of the Christian Uighurs, and the above general Tsz-i, defended the Emperor against the rebellion of An-Lu-shan (Saeki, *ibid.*), p. 231).

Having identified with some degree of probability one of the four Christian Turkish kings mentioned in the document, we will now venture to advance a step further and try to clear up the question of their number. On pp. 316-317 we have endeavoured to show that there were four powerful confederacies of Turco-Tartar tribes who had to a great extent adopted Christianity: the Keraits, the Uighurs, the Naimans, and the Merkites. Is it possible to suppose that each one of the above kings was the Khāḳān of one of these tribes? If the author is treating of the subject chronologically, as he appears to be doing, so that all his four Christian kings are to be considered as more or less contemporaries, this hypothesis would at least have the advantage of solving those difficulties of his document which fall under the domain of history. If the Christianism of the Merkites comes to be considered not thoroughly established we would propose, in order to complete the number four, the Uriyān-gaḳit spoken of on p. 337.

In the ensuing pages we give the translation of all the document as found in the MS. and the text of that part of it only which deals with the Christian Turks.

III.

Translation.

The letter of Mar Philoxenus of Mabbūg sent by him to Abi 'Afr, military Governor of Ḥirta of Nu'mān, in which is contained the story of the accursed and anathematised Nestorius.

To the one who is noble, pure, and God loving, like Abraham; to the one who gives his wealth in alms to the poor, like Job; to the one who delivers the lambs bought with the blood of Christ from the heresy of the Nestorians which is a second Jezebel, like Obadiah: Abi 'Afr, the military Governor of Ḥirta of Nu'mān; from Philoxenus, Bishop of Mabbūg, many greetings in God Jesus Christ.

Because you asked me in your letter to inform you of what has been established in the Church of the Greeks by the holy Doctors, I write you what follows and bring to your notice the fact that the holy

Fathers gathered together from time to time and threw away false heresies from the Church of God.

In the days of the Emperor Hadrian Sabellius rose against the Church of God, and he blasphemed and said that there was only one person in the Trinity, and because of that Mary was the mother of the Trinity, and passion, death and crucifixion belonged to the Trinity, and that the Body and the Blood which we receive from the altar were of the Trinity. Forty-three Bishops assembled in Ancyra of Galatia, and anathematised from the Church of God the feeble-minded Sabellius because he did not wish to recant his impiety.

In the days of the Emperor Valerianus Paul of Samosata rose against the Church of God, and called the living Son of God a just man only, like one of those just men that were in the world before Him. The Bishops gathered together at Antioch and anathematised Paul of Samosata, and threw him away from the Church of God because he did not wish to recant.

In the days of the victorious Emperor Constantine the accursed serpent Arius rose against the Church of God, and called the Son of God a creature. Three hundred and eighteen Fathers congregated in Nicæa and anathematised Arius and drove him out of the Church of God, because he did not desist from his impiety. These holy Fathers established the true faith and laid down various Canons.

In the days of Constantine the younger [1] Eusebius of Cæsarea rose against the Church of God, and he foolishly pretended that the Son of God was younger than His Father. Sixty Bishops assembled in Rome in order to drive Eusebius out of the Church of God, and they rose and anathematised his opinion. He recanted the false opinions whereby he had blasphemed against the living Son of God, showed penitence, and subscribed to the true doctrines; whereupon the Orthodox Fathers received him into the holy Church of the true God.

In the days of Theodosius the Great Macedonius rose against the Church of God, and called the Holy Spirit a creature, and a hundred and fifty Bishops assembled in Constantinople, the Metropolis, and anathematised Macedonius, because he did not wish to turn away from the false opinions that he was holding.

And there was a man called Addai, from the town of Germanicia,

[1] The Syrians call by this name the Emperor Constantius.

which is Mar'ash. He was (originally) from Atak, a village situated in the proximity of the town of Dara, and the name of his wife was 'Amalka. It happened that this Addai quarrelled with a pregnant woman from the above village of Atak, and he lifted his hand and struck her; this immediately caused the abortion of a boy, who died; and the mother also was brought near her death. Then Addai rose forthwith and left his village, and took his wife and fled to the country of the Ṣuphananians, which is the country of Hataka. They remained there a short time, then they quitted it, and went and lived in the town of Samosata in which they took domicile. Two boys were born to them in this town; they called the first Ba'ilshmīn,[1] and the second Abi'ashūm. After a while Addai and his wife died and they were buried in the same town of Samosata.

After the death of their parents, Addai and his wife, the boys rose and went to Germanicia which is Mar'ash, where they lived and married. A boy was born to Ba'ilshmin, and he called him Theodore, while Abi'ashūm gave the name of Nestorius to a son that he had. When the boys grew up the parents sent them to school to learn Greek, and they thoroughly mastered this language.

Then both of them rose and went and entered Athens, the city of philosophers, in order to learn philosophy. Now the sons of the nobles of the city of Constantinople were their fellow-students there, and these praised and extolled the wisdom and the philosophy of Theodore and Nestorius before the Emperor Honorius Cesar, who ordered both of them to repair to Antioch in order to meet the Patriarch and be ordained Bishops: Nestorius to Constantinople, and Theodore to Mopsuestia. When they were ordained Bishops and each went to his see then both of them began to corrupt the true doctrine preached to us by Prophets, Apostles, and Fathers, and in their homilies they subtly divided the Only Begotten Son of God into two natures.

In the seven Discourses that Theodore sent to Nestorius and Nestorius to Theodore, the latter wrote that Jesus Christ was a man created in Mary, the Holy Virgin, by the will of the Holy Trinity, as Adam was created at the beginning from earth without human intercourse; and because God the Word dwelt in Him from time to

[1] The Syriac word for *Jupiter;* lit. "the Master of Heavens."

time as if in a holy prophet, we must resort to distinctions (in Him) and introduce different attributes for each nature, in a way that conception, birth, baptism and all the other points of the Dispensation should belong to the man who was born of Mary, and that powers, miracles, wonders, and prodigies should belong to the Word God who was from time to time dwelling in Him. This is the faith of impiety which Theodore sent to Nestorius, and concerning it both were in perfect agreement.

When the believing Emperor Honorius, worthy of good memory, died, he was succeeded by Theodosius the younger, and then the two accursed and anathematised hawks, Nestorius and Theodore, began to divulge openly the falsehood of their doctrine. But when the victorious Emperor Theodosius became aware of the fact that they were both of them contradicting the tenets of the true faith, he gave orders and two hundred and twenty Bishops assembled concerning them in the town of Ephesus. And Nestorius sent to Theodore while in Mopsuestia his eighth Discourse in which he wrote :—

"O brother, go to the Council of Ephesus and anathematise me ; and be not grieved, O brother, in anathematising me before that Council, while in thy heart thou remainest steadfast in (our) belief, and thou teachest it to the children of the Church to the measure of thy capacity. Indeed '*anathema*' is not of one kind only in the Holy Scripture. Our Lord testifies to this by saying 'He who loves me keeps my commandments' (John xiv. 15) and the Apostle Paul said : 'He who does not love our Lord Jesus Christ let him be *anathema*'[1] (1 Cor. xvi. 22). This kind of *anathema* is spread and extended on all men, who do not keep the commandments of our Lord, as He Himself said. There is also another kind of *anathema* spoken of by the Apostle Paul : 'Though an angel from heaven preach unto you more than we have preached unto you let him be *anathematised* by the Church' (Gal. i. 8). From this kind of '*anathema*' flee, O brother, and if possible, let it not be even spoken of with thy lips. Further, God said to the prophet Moses : 'All the "*anathemas*" of the children of Israel shall be to Aaron and his sons' (Lev. vi. 20 ; Numb. viii. 19) ; these '*anathemas*' mean here ex-votos and offerings. And Jesus, son of Nūn, says thus : 'Everything

[1] The word "anathema" (*ḥirma*) is used in the Syriac Bible in this and in all the following quotations.

there is in this town of Jericho, is "*anathema*" to the Lord,' (Josh. vi. 17) that is to say an offering to the Lord or an ex-voto. And the Apostle Paul says in another place: 'I could wish that I myself should be "*anathema*" for my brethren and kinsmen who are the children of Israel' (Rom. ix. 3). Anathematise me, therefore, O brother, in the sense in which Paul was wishing to be an offering to the children of his people, and be not grieved."

When the Council of two hundred and twenty decreed and anathematised Nestorius, Theodore also anathematised him, but in the meaning which Nestorius had shown to him. And when the Council broke up and everybody returned to his country and his place, the wretched Theodore began to introduce into the Church the teaching of Nestorius which he had previously embraced, and he wrote the hymn called "the Epiphany of the King" in which he contradicted the Church in teaching openly four persons in the Trinity. So far as the Christ is concerned he holds and believes Him to be a mere man, in saying thus: "Thy stature, O Christ, was smaller than that of the children of Jacob who sinned against the Father who elected Thee, and who kindled the wrath of the Eternal Son who dwelt in Thee, and who angered the Holy Spirit who Sanctified Thee." And again: "Blessed is God the Word who came down and put on the Christ, the second Adam, and made Him (as innocent) as a child, in the water of baptism." And again in another place: "The Holy Spirit came to-day (on Him?) because He made the young David flee (before His innocence?)."[1]

It is obvious that he preached four persons in that unholy hymn called "the Epiphany of the King." He also wrote the divisions of the headings of the Psalms in order to deceive the remote Churches and detach them from the truth of their faith in order to bring them to his impure interpretation. Indeed he said to the simple-minded (among them): "My brethren, you ought to believe in Christ who taught us to glorify the Trinity;" and by his craftiness he made this (fourth) person as a crown to prayer, because at the end of it he taught them to utter the following: "Thanks to the One who opened our mouths to glorify night and day the Lord of all time, who is the nature of the Holy Trinity: Father, Son, and Holy Spirit.[2]

[1] This short line culled from its context is difficult to understand.

[2] The first words of this sentence are found in the *Breviarium Chaldaicum*, ii. 75.

We, the children of the true faith will anathematise all who have subscribed and subscribe to this impure doctrine, and will confess and glorify the Holy Trinity as One ; may it be exalted now and for ever and ever ! Amen. And we will reject all who profess the quaternity of the Emperor Valens (or Valentinian). And Theodore also was rejected from the Holy Church.

In the days of the Emperor Marcian, Eutyches rose against the Holy Church, and said that the body of the Son of God came down with Him from heaven. Five hundred and sixty seven Bishops assembled to reject Eutyches from the Church of God. When Leo of Rome heard this, he sent to them an epistle (suggesting to them) to receive Nestorius and his impure interpretations. Soon after the epistle of Leo, the accursed, the anathematised, and the impure Patriarch[1] of Rome, was read ; on hearing it the Emperor Marcian sent to them a letter intimating that all those who refused to accept all that was in the *tomos* of Leo should leave their chairs and sit on the ground ; and because they loved their chairs, they transgressed the vows with which they had bound themselves thirty-six times, and they rashly disregarded the anathemas of the Holy Fathers, and subscribed to the *tomos* of Leo. They all remained in their chairs except Dioscorus, Patriarch of Alexandria, who by his own free will rose up and sat on the ground ; and because he did not subscribe to them they sent the Saint of God Mar Dioscorus to exile, and they locked him up in the town of Gangra, and in his place they promoted Proterius his syncellus, that is to say his secretary, to the see of Alexandria.

When the inhabitants of Alexandria heard what took place, they dispatched a missive to the Council of Chalcedon (addressed) to the Emperor Marcian in which they wrote : " You have done well, and we subscribe to what you have done ; " but those priests, deacons, and laymen who did not subscribe to what was decreed by the Council of Chalcedon, rose up and took Timothy, the disciple of Dioscorus, and fled to Abyssinia (*Kush*). And Proterius the syncellus, who had become Patriarch in the place of Dioscorus, his master, entered the town of Alexandria by means of secular power and tyrannic

[1] In the text through the copyist's error *malka*, "Emperor." See below.

sword, and he, together with the Bishops who followed him tyrannically governed the flock of Christ, and did not recoil even before murder and the shedding of blood, so much so that this same Proterius, the syncellus, who became Patriarch, killed through Roman soldiers twenty-four thousand men, most of whom were Bishops, monks, priests and deacons.

Soon after, however, the inhabitants of Alexandria, stirred up with the zeal of God, entered his house, stoned him, killed him, dragged him out, and threw him into the sea. When the priests, the deacons, and the laymen that had fled from Alexandria with Timothy, disciple of Dioscorus, heard that the accursed syncellus was dead, they returned and implored the faithful Bishops to elect Timothy their Patriarch, because they had heard that the holy Dioscorus had died in exile in Gangra. The Bishops of Abyssinia rose then and elected Timothy their Patriarch, but he feared to go to Alexandria because it came to his knowledge that the Emperor Marcian was still alive.

When the Emperor Marcian died, and was succeeded on the throne by Leo, then Timothy rose and entered Alexandria, and sat on the throne of Dioscorus, his master. All Alexandria then flocked, subscribed, and bowed to him; and he prayed and absolved the inhabitants of Alexandria, because they showed repentance to God. Some men, however, among those priests, deacons, and laymen who had fled with Timothy to Abyssinia, did not wish to receive into their communion the inhabitants of Alexandria, and contended that all those who had subscribed in any shape or form to the Council of Chalcedon, neither priesthood nor baptism remained to them, and the Holy Spirit did not come down to bless their Sacrifice in their Churches. On receiving this news, four wretched priests, lawyers by profession (*nōmīkē*), took the Gospel and placed it on the head of the monk Isaiah, and they elected him their Bishop; from that day down to our own time, they have been called "*Isaians Acephali.*"

Because your Excellency[1] wrote in your second letter and asked me concerning these *Acephali*, whether they were professing rightly or not, I wrote and narrated to you their story, as I learned it from the books of the Holy Fathers. And the Holy Council of the three hundred and eighteen[2] has decreed that if any one belonging to (the

[1] I.e. Abu 'Afr. [2] I.e. of Nicæa.

heresy of) Paul of Samosata returns from his error and comes to the true faith, let him first be baptised and afterwards he may partake of the Eucharist with the children of the Holy Church. The reason for which the holy Council published this decree concerning the Eucharist is that (the followers of Paul of Samosata) had twisted the truth, and openly taught then—as they do till now—their false teaching. The Apostle Paul bears witness to this by saying: "If the root be holy, the branches also are holy" (Rom. xi. 16), and these are the baptism and the ordination of the Chalcedonians.

If one asserts by mistake and says that among them there were holy, pious, and just men, and because of this all should not be anathematised, let such a one remember the story of Lot, and let him see, examine, and consider that although he was the only just man found in all Sodom, God did not leave him to perish with the wicked and perverse Sodomites, but took him out towards the mountain. What happened in Sodom happened also in Chalcedon in which the unholy Council was held, and in which (the Bishops) trod on the anathemas of the Holy Fathers; one man, however, was saved in it: the holy Dioscorus, Patriarch of Alexandria, who shook off their dust from him and confessed and said: "I shall never have a share and participation of any kind with you." In this way also the Egyptian monks assembled and anathematised the Council of Chalcedon, and they consumed it with the fire of their anathemas so that it should never bear any fruits.

The wife of Lot left Sodom while her heart was in it; and God forgave her in order that she may repent; but when she persisted with stubbornness in her bad inclinations, she turned and looked back with a perverse desire, and instantly the severe punishment of God overtook her, and she became a pillar of salt. If because she turned and looked back she became a pillar of salt, to what severe punishment and perdition will come those who subscribe to the wicked and perverse Council of Chalcedon? And those who openly proclaim the name of one of those blasphemers who are covered with anathemas and curses, are to be called not only blasphemers but also persecutors of God.

When Paul used formerly to persecute and fight the churches of God, it was not said of him that he persecuted men, but God said to him: "Saul, Saul, why persecutest thou me? And he answered and said, 'Who art thou, Lord?' I know not. And God said in a voice from heaven, 'I am Jesus of Nazareth whom thou persecutest.'" (Acts ix. 4-5). It is, however, clear that Paul was persecuting the Apostles and not God. He who, therefore, persecutes the saints, persecutes God. When the priest prays on the altar, the Holy Spirit comes down and sanctifies the mysteries, and changes them into the body and the blood of God ; the contrary would be the case if the name of one of those blasphemers of the unholy, wicked, and perverse Council of Chalcedon, was invoked.

A great number of people deviated from the path of truth, and became Nestorians, on account of the severity of the persecution and oppression. And the Nestorians had for head an ungodly Catholicos, called Aḳāḳ, from whose time dates the Nestorian Catholicate in Ctesiphon.[1] And there had been in Ctesiphon another wicked man, a certain Papa, who also from fear of the sword became pagan and deviated from the truth.[2]

At that time some men from the Turks[3] who are Christians came to Ctesiphon from the remote countries in order to elect a Metropolitan for themselves, and have him ordained, as was their wont ; because it

[1] Aḳāḳ (Acacius) was Patriarch or Catholicos of the Eastern Church from 485 to 496. He was, as the author states, the first Nestorian Patriarch. Cf. Labourt, *Le Christianisme*, p. 145 *sq*.

[2] Papa was Patriarch from about A.D. 290 to 328. He was the first Catholicos in the series of the Patriarchs of the East after the Council of Nicæa. The author writes of him that he turned pagan, but this is a biased Jacobite judgment upon the trouble that he had with some Bishops of the Persian Empire who refused to acknowledge his jurisdiction based on the innovation of his elevation to the Patriarchate through the intermediary of Constantine and the Bishops of the Roman Empire. The best and earliest account of him is undoubtedly that of Mshīḥa-Zkha in my *Sources Syriaques*, i. pp. 119-123, where I have also analysed in the footnotes all the previously known sources.

[3] According to Rockhill (*in op. suprà laud.*, p. 109) the earliest mention of the "Turks" is found in the *Chou shu* (A.D. 557-581). In the Syriac chronicle which we quoted above (p. 305), and which was written not later than 680, the word Ṭurkāyé, "Turks," occurs as a well-known name. Further, according to *Thesaurus Syr.* (col. 1453), the name is used in *Kal.* and *Dimn.* of Būd, who died not much later than A.D. 570. The Syriac sources seem to be earlier than the Chinese ones in the use of the name. See also the history of the Syriac writer John of Ephesus who died in 586 (3rd part, book vi. ch. vi. and xxiii. etc.), where the name appears as *Ṭurḳis*. Many Syriac authors call the Turks "Huns" or "Sons of Ṁagog".

was in Ctesiphon that the consecration of their Metropolitans used to take place. Each one of their countries had one Metropolitan, after the ordination of whom they repaired to their land. And the above Papa of Ctesiphon used to receive ordination from (the Patriarch) of Antioch. And at that time when those Christian Turks came to receive ordination according to their habit, they discovered that Aḳāḳ was not under the jurisdiction of the Patriarch of Antioch, but that he had rebelled against him and was a heretic ; thereupon they became angry with him, refused to receive ordination from him, and returned to their country in great grief.

After a time they were in great distress, because they had no Metropolitan, and so they came back and repaired as far as Ctesiphon, having it meantime in their mind to reach Antioch and have an interview with the Patriarch. On the score of the length of the journey, however, and because of strifes, conflicts, and wars, that raged at that time between Powers, they found themselves unable to proceed to Antioch, but remained five years in Ctesiphon, in the hope that there would be peace and the roads would be open again for traffic. At the end they lost heart and courage, and not willing to return to their country empty handed as on the first occasion, and noticing that it was too late in the season to dally, they went to Aḳāḳ, the Catholicos of the Nestorians, and discussed with him the reason of his revolt against the authority of the Patriarch of Antioch.

Then the heretic Aḳāḳ, in conjunction with those who followed his perverse opinions, deceived with their cunning those simple and unsophisticated folk and answered them : "It is not on account of faith that we have separated ourselves from the Patriarch of Antioch and raised a Catholicos, but it is because of the peril to all the Christians of the East,—that will ensue from a visit to Antioch, which will be interpreted as an act of disloyalty to the temporal rulers,—that we do not go there.[1] Further, we established a Catholicos for ourselves on

[1] The author is here repeating the gist of the Oriental tradition to the effect that the Catholicos of the East was ordained and given spiritual jurisdiction by the Patriarch of Antioch. Every time, tradition tells us, that a Patriarch was elected in the East prior to the spread of Nestorianism, he had to repair to Antioch for the purpose above mentioned. It was only through lack of safety in the roads due to political troubles between the Persian and the Byzantine empires, that the Patriarch of Antioch relaxed his hold of his eastern colleague (Māri, *loc. cit.* p. 5 ; 'Amr, *loc. cit.* p. 4 ; Barhebraeus,

account of wars, conflicts, and strifes that are raging in our countries; and because we did that we live now in peace and security." By such crooked words those simple and unsophisticated folk were deceived, and received ordination from the Nestorians, and they were given a Metropolitan from the Nestorians by false pretences, while they were unaware of their deception, and of the falsehood of their abominable beliefs. And this habit is handed down to them to the present day, because any time their Bishop dies they come to the Nestorians, and take another one to replace him from Ctesiphon. The see (of their Bishop ?) is in the pagan town which we have mentioned above,[1] and it is he who ordains for them priests and deacons.

These Christian Turks eat meat and drink milk. They do not put any difference between lawful and unlawful food, but eat everything in good and pure concience. By such acts they are believed by outsiders to be unclean, while in reality they are not. All their habits are clean, and their beliefs are orthodox and true like our own. Although they receive their ordination from the Nestorians, they do it *bonâ fide*, while unaware of their guile, falsehood, and wickedness. They believe in one glorious nature in the Holy Trinity, and like us they hold to three adorable Persons, and profess that the Divine

Chron. Eccl., ii. 26; Assemani, *Bibl. Orient.*, iii. 51 *sq.*). There seems to be some truth in this legend, about which, however, Mshīḥa-Zkha knows nothing at all. The most ancient Syriac writer who does make mention of it is John of Phenek who was writing about 690 (pp. 123-124 of the text; in vol. ii. of our *Sources Syriaques*) and it is somewhat astonishing that no ecclesiastical historian who wrote on the subject has noticed it since it was published in 1908. Here is a translation of the whole passage referring to the legend, which places the incident about the beginning of the reign of Sapor II. (309-379): "At a time preceding this the rights of the Patriarchal see of Syria were transferred to the Church of Kōkê (Ctesiphon) in the East, on account of the enmity existing between the Empires of the East and of the West, which were at war every day. Many Bishops were killed when repairing from here to there, and from there to here, on account of the remoteness of the Patriarch. They accused them of being spies, while in reality they did it because of their thirst for the blood of the saints. And the Father-Bishops, in grief for the murder of their colleagues, ordained that the Patriarch of the Church of Kōkê should have full jurisdiction over the Bishops of the East, according to the enactments of ecclesiastical Canons."

[1] The author has not mentioned above the name of the Turkish town. See *Foreword*, p. 348. This "pagan town" appears to me to refer to Baghdad, the capital of the "pagan" Muslims.

Word, one of these three Persons of the Holy Trinity suffered, died, and was crucified, and by His death and His resurrection He saved us. This is their true faith.

Any one they see circumcised like pagans[1] they kill immediately, and they carry with them their sanctuaries anywhere they depart after their halts. Their feasts they celebrate with great pomp, and they love more than any other people the commemorations of saints and martyrs. They do not learn nor do they accept any other script besides our own, and in the language of us Syrians they write and read the Books of the two Testaments: the Old and the New, and the writings of the Orthodox Fathers. In their gatherings they translate the above Books into their Turkish language, while they never venture to change into the Turkish language the adorable name of our Divine Lord Jesus Christ nor that of Mary, the mother of God, but they pronounce them as they are in our Syriac language.[2] As to the rest of the words and names they render them into the Turkish language, in order that all their congregation may understand what is read.

In the days of the holy Lent they do not eat fresh and new meat, but meat that is dry like wood;[3] and they fast from evening till evening, and they make the wafers of the Holy and Divine Sacrament from bread of pure wheat. They bring from other countries, with great care and diligence, pure flour from pure wheat, and they store it up for the purpose; so also they fetch from remote regions the raisins from which they make the wine used for the Holy Communion.

[1] This may refer to the Jews, and in case the document was written after the Arab invasion, to the Muslims. I firmly believe, however, that the document was written after the Arab invasion, and that the mention of Circumcision refers here to Muslims. Circumcision has apparently never been practised by ancient Turks and Mongols. "The Indo-Germanic peoples, the Mongols, and the Finno-Ugric races (except where they have been influenced by Muḥammadanism) alone are entirely unacquainted with Circumcision" (Hastings' *Encyclopædia of Religion and Ethics*, iii. 659).

[2] This information is confirmed by the Soghdian documents discovered in Central Asia. See *Foreword.*

[3] This information is corroborated by Friar William (*ibid.* p. 64): "So then if it happens that an ox or a horse dies, they dry its flesh by cutting it into narrow strips and hanging it in the sun and the wind where at once and without salt it becomes dry without any evil smell." And Rockhill adds in a footnote: "Sun-dried meat is used in Mongolia and among the nomads of Tibet. It is usually eaten without any other preparation."

In their dresses they do not differ from the Turks who are pagan. All the people of the town speak another language called Yabatai,[1] and their script is in their own language. From there Eastwards, to the distance of two months' journey, there are many towns that contain pagan Turks who worship idols, and have script in their own language. The border town is called Ḳaragur[am],[2] and the name of its King is Idi-Ḳut.[3] Five days' journey from there lies the habitat of the Turks who are Christians and of whom we spoke above. They are true believers and God-fearing folk, and they dwell under tents, and have no towns, no villages, and no houses; but they are divided into powerful and great clans, who journey from place to place.

They have many possessions: sheep, cattle, camels, and horses. Each camel of theirs has two humps like a Salm[4] (?) They have four great and powerful kings, each one living farther from the other, whose names are: the first Gawirk,[5] the second Girk,[6] the third

[1] Is it possible that this word is connected in any way with "Chagatai" the old dialect of the Turkic group of languages?

[2] I believe that this *Ḳaragur* is a copyist's error for *Karaḳuram* or Ḳaraḳurum. At the end of the Syriac word there is a partly obliterated letter which appears to have been a *mīm*. In the second half of the eighth Christian century (i.e. the time in which we believe that the document was written) the Christian Uighur Turks were all-powerful in Eastern Asia and had their capital at Ḳaraḳurum. Howorth's *History of the Mongols*, i. 21.

[3] As stated in the text *Idi-Ḳut* was the nickname of all the kings of the Uighur Turks. Juwaini expressly states in his *Tārīkh-i Jahān-Gushā* (i. 32, Gibb Mem.), that the Uighur Turks called their kings by this name, which means "Lord of the Kingdom." Barhebraeus (*Chron. Syr.*, p. 427, edit. Bedjan) asserts also the same thing. In his *Chron. Arab.* (edit. of the Jesuits of Beirut, 1890, pp. 399 and 402), the word is wrongly spelt *Idi-Ḳūb*. See also Rashīd's *Jāmi' at-Tawārīkh*, *ibid.* p. 298, etc.

[4] Is it possible that this word is the Arabic *sanim*, "big-humped" camel?

[5] The name is tentatively identified in the *Foreword*, p. 351. We may here compare for a certain similarity in the names of later generations: *Gaur-Khan*, which was used as a title of the kings of Ḳara-Khitai Turks and Tartars inhabiting Eastern Turkestan. See Juwaini (*Tārīkh-i Jahān Gushā*, Gibb Mem.), i. 46-48, 52, 56, 57, and cf. also Guyuk, the grandson of Chingis Khan (Barhebraeus, *Chron. Syr.*, *ibid.* p. 481). Juwaini (*ibid.* ii. 86), says that the word means "King of Kings."

[6] The name is tentatively identified in the *Foreword*. We may here compare for a certain similarity in the names of later generations: *Garik*, or *Charīk*, son of Chūchi Khān (Rashīd's *Jāmi' at-Tawārīkh*, p. 115 (*ibid.*)). Cf. also *Churīka*, son of Tūli (*ibid.*), p. 200.

Ṭāsahz,[1] and the fourth Langu.[2] They have a name common to all: Tātar,[3] and the name of their country is Sericon.[4] It is said that each one of these kings has with him four hundred thousand families, when they congregate at the time of their halts. Their country is broad and reaches as far as Magog,[5] the city of the pagans, and beyond them everybody is heathen. But the Christian Turks of whom we have spoken receive ordination from the Bishop whose see is in that large town of the pagans[6] which has five big churches.

These Christian Turks dwell under tents and pavilions, and have from themselves priests, deacons, and monks. They have many places of worship with them in their pavilions, and they ring the bells and read the Books in our Syriac tongue. They celebrate like us all the Festivals of the Dispensation of our Saviour and Lord Jesus Christ.

[1] The name is identified in the *Foreword*, p. 351. For a certain similarity in the names of later generations we may compare *Tāisi* the Mongolian Emir and general spoken of by Juwaini in his *Tārīkh-i Jahān-Gushā* (Gibb Mem.), i. pp. 113, 128, 136. Cf. also in Rashīd's *Jāmi'* (*ibid.* p. 466) "Tāishi" who proclaimed himself King of North China, and *ibid.*, p. 584.

[2] The name has been tentatively identified in the *Foreword*, p. 351; it can be illustrated by scores of North Chinese vocables, some of which may be seen in the excellent index to Yule-Cordier's *Cathay*, 1916, iv. pp. 318-320.

[3] The earliest date to which the name *Tatar* has so far been traced is A.D. 732. Mention is made of *Toḳuz Tatar* "nine (tribes of) Tatars" in a Turkish inscription found on the river Orkhon and bearing that date. See Thomsen, *Inscriptions de l'Orkhon*, 98, 126, 140, and Rockhill, *op. cit.*, p. 113. How far the word *T'atun* can refer to *Tatar* or is to be identified with it is discussed by Cordier in his *Notes and Addenda* to Yule's edition of Marco Polo, 1920, p. 55.

[4] Is the name *Serīcon* related in any way to the *Sarīks*, those Turkish tribes now living in the neighbourhood of Panjdeh and Yulatan, but whose former habitat was central Turkestan? That *Sericon* is to be identified with *Seres* and *Serike* of Ptolemy is discussed in the "Foreword," pp. 326-327.

[5] The Geography of the document has been rendered still more confused by the use of the word *Magog* which was often employed by both Eastern and Western writers to denote almost any Central Asian country of which little was known. Barhebraeus in his *Chron. Syr.*, sometimes calls the Empire of the Mongols that of the "Magogians," and on p. 579 (edit. Bedjan), he writes of the Emperor Kaigatu, "And when he was surely established as the head of the Empire of Magog." The author does not know the name of Mongolia and North China or Cathay, but applies to both of them the name *Sericon*, the appellation by which they are known in Ptolemy's geographical work. Michael the Syrian calls constantly the Turks as "people of Magog" (i. 103; iii. 149 and 222, etc.).

[6] We believe that the allusion is to Baghdad.

They do not practise circumcision like pagans, but are baptised like us with the holy baptism and the holy chrism. They believe that Mary is the mother of God, and profess that Christ is God. They keep the Festivals and the Sundays like all other Christians.

No bread at all is found in their country, no cornfield, no vineyard, no wine, and no raisins; and all their food consists of meat and milk of sheep; and they have a great quantity of flocks.[1]

The occasion of this arose at the time when persecution was aflame against the Christians of the countries of the Persians, at the hand of the accursed Barṣauli[2] of Nisibin, who killed seven thousand priests, monks, and clerics, and an innumerable multitude of believing

[1] This information about the food of the Turks and Tartars is well attested in history. See the Syriac authors quoted in the *Foreword*. For Western writers we will only refer to Friar William's account in Rockhill (*op. cit.* pp. 62-63): "They drink great quantities of mare's milk, if they have it; they drink also sheep's, goat's, cow's and camel's milk. Wine they have not unless it is sent from other nations or is given to them. . . . Of their food and victuals you must know that they eat all their dead animals without distinction, and with such flocks and herds it cannot be but that many animals die."—Pian de Carpine writes also: "They have no bread nor oil nor vegetables, nothing but meat, of which, however, they eat so little that other people could scarcely exist on it" (*ibid.* pp. 63-64). See also Barhebraeus, *Chron. Syr.*, pp. 408-409. Juwaini, *Jahān Gushā* i. 15, writes: "Their food was flesh of dogs and mice and other dead carrion, and their drink was milk of animals (*bahāim*)." Michael the Syrian (iii. 152) says: "They slaughter and eat all that moves on the earth: domestic animals, savage beasts, reptiles, insects, and birds. They eat also dead carrion."

[2] The copyist writes the name of the famous Barṣauma, Bishop of Nisibin, in a derisive way, as Barṣaula. The same thing is done by the copyist of Barhebraeus's Ecclesiastical history (*Chron. Eccles.*, ii. 69). Further, Barhebraeus (*ibid.*) puts the number of the faithful done to death by Barṣauma at 7700, while the author of the present document counts 7000 priests, monks, and clerics, and an innumerable multitude of laymen. This fantastic travesty of the history of the introduction of Nestorianism into the Persian Empire has been well exposed by J. Labourt (*Christianisme dans l'Empire Perse*, p. 134 *sq.*). By hatred for the memory of Barṣauma his name is written very often as "Barṣaula" by modern Jacobite scribes, and it is also as often as not written upside down like the name of "Satan". It is purely an affair of the copyists, and has absolutely nothing to do with the writers whose books they transcribe. Shammas Matti, the well-known Jacobite copyist of the present MS., assured me verbally that he has always written, and he will always write, the name of Barṣauma in this way, even if he was transcribing a Nestorian MS. What other means have we, said he, to distinguish this Barṣauma from our Saint Barṣauma?

laymen. It is because of this that the Holy Spirit does not come down to sanctify the sacrament (= the Eucharist) of the Nestorian heretics. Since it has been made known that the Holy Spirit does not come down and sanctify the Sacrament of these heretics, the spirit that comes down on their altars and their sacrament is, therefore, that of Satan. And as those who were baptised by Judas Iscariot, before his fall, were truly baptised, because of the truth that he was proclaiming, so also are those who took part in the unholy Synod of Chalcedon. Indeed, before they blasphemed and took part in it the Spirit used to come down on them, on their sacrament, and on their altars, but after they blasphemed and rent asunder the true faith, and went out of the fold of life, they became anathematised and rejected, ceased to possess the Holy Spirit, and have only the spirit of error and of Satan. They also were deprived and dispossessed of baptism, ordination, and of all the sacraments of the Holy Church. May the Lord God deliver us together with all the children of the Holy Church from any intercourse and communion with them, through the intercession of Mary, the mother of God, and of all the saints! Glory be to God! and may His grace and mercy be upon all of us! Amen.

Here ends the letter of Mar Philoxenus, Bishop of Mabbūg, to Abi 'Afr, Military Governor of Hīrta of Nu'mān.

SUPPLEMENTARY NOTE (to pp. 323 and 325).

According to Ibn aṭ-Ṭayib who died in 1043 (see Vat. MS. Borgia 153 fol. 198b in Sachau's *Ausb.*, p. 24) the Bishoprics of Meru, Herat, Samarḳand, India, and China were elevated to the rank of Archbishoprics at a much earlier date: Meru by the Patriarch Isaac (399-410) and the rest by the Patriarch Ishō'-Yahb (628-643). China and Samarḳand might have been, therefore, the seats not only of Bishops but of Archbishops more than a century before the time that we were disposed to assign to them.

... ܘܥܒܕ ܠܗܘܢ ܠܡܫܬܘܬܦ̈ܐ ܚܣܝܐ ܩܐܬܘܠܝܩܐ ܟܘܠܐ ܕܥܡܗ ܗ̇ܘܐ ܐܘܦ
ܕܡܟܢܗ ܘܠܟܠ ܦܪܝܫ ܩܐܬܘܠܝܩܘܬܐ ܕܝܠܗܘܢ ܕܡܫܬܘܬܦ̈ܐ ܒܦܬܓܡܝܗܘܢ.
ܘܐܝܬ ܗ̇ܘܐ ܚܕ ܦܓܥܐ ܒܦܬܓܡܝܗܘܢ ܕܐܦ ܗ̇ܘ ܕܥܠ ܡܢ ܕܡܫܠܛܐ ܕܡܫܒܚܐ
ܐܣܩ ܘܫܠܚ ܡܢ ܦܓܪܐ. ܘܒܗ ܒܗ̇ܘ ܙܒܢܐ ܐܬܘ ܐܢܫܐ ܡܢ ܬܘܪܟܝܐ
ܦܢܘ ܒܪܡܫܐ ܡܢ ܐܬܪܘܬܐ ܚܢ̈ܦܐ ܕܢܫܒܘܢ ܠܗܘܢ ܫܒܝܐ ܐܝܟ ܘܢܒܙܘܢ
ܠܗܘܢ ܡܬܪܘܦܦܠܢܝܬܐ ܠܟܠ ܐܬܪܐ ܚܕ ܡܬܪܘܦܦܠܢܝܬܐ ܘܐܝܟܢ ܠܟܢܘܫܬܗܘܢ.
ܗܘ ܕܝܢ ܦܓܪܐ ܕܦܬܓܡܝܗܘܢ ܡܢ ܗ̇ܘ ܕܐܬܚܣܢ ܡܫܡܫ ܗ̇ܘܐ ܫܡܫܐ ܐܝܟ
ܕܟܗܢܘܬܐ. ܘܒܬܪ ܚܕ ܙܒܢܐ ܬܘܒ ܗܠܝܢ ܬܘܪܟܝܐ ܕܒܪܡܫܐ ܕܢܫܒܘܢ ܫܡܫܐ
ܐܝܟ ܕܟܗܢܘܬܐ ܐܝܟ ܕܒܝܬܗܘܢ ܘܐܫܟܚܘܗܝ ܠܐܦܐ ܕܠܐ ܐܝܬܘܗܝ ܬܘܒ ܚܝܐ
ܡܫܠܛܢܐ ܕܦܬܓܡܐ ܗܘ ܕܐܬܚܣܢ ܐܠܐ ܕܐܝܬܘܗܝ ܡܫܪܐ ܒܠܘܬܗܘܢ ܐܦ
ܐܪܬܘܕܘܟܣܐ. ܘܐܬܒܠܥ ܒܗ ܘܠܐ ܙܟܐ ܕܢܬܒܠܥ ܡܢܗ ܫܡܫܐ ܐܝܟ
ܕܟܗܢܘܬܐ ܐܠܐ ܗܦܟܘ ܠܗܘܢ ܠܐܬܪܗܘܢ ܒܒܪܝܬܐ ܢܦܠܐ. ܘܒܬܪ ܙܒܢܐ
ܦܝܫ ܕܐܬܐܠܘ ܡܠܟܐ ܕܝܠܗ ܗ̇ܘܐ ܠܗܘܢ ܚܝܠ ܒܫܢܝܐ ܠܘܬ ܗܦܟܘ
ܗ̇ܢܘܢ ܘܫܡܠܦܘ ܠܗܘܢ ܕܢܦܩ ܠܦܬܓܡܝܗܘܢ ܘܫܩܠܘ ܒܐܝܕܝܗܘܢ ܕܢܦܩܘܢ
ܠܐܬܚܣܢ ܠܘܬ ܦܬܓܡܐ ܘܡܢ ܟܠܗ ܢܣܝܘܢܐ ܕܐܘܪܚܐ ܘܡܢ ܫܪܟܐ ܘܫܒܝܐ
ܘܡܪܚܐ ܕܐܝܬ ܗ̇ܘܐ ܒܗܝܢ ܡܠܟܘܬܐ ܒܗܘ ܙܒܢܐ ܠܐ ܐܬܡܠܟܘ ܕܢܐܬܘܢ
ܠܐܬܚܣܢܐ. ܘܒܬܪ ܗ̇ܢܘܢ ܒܦܬܓܡܝܗܘܢ ܡܠܟܐ ܕܫܠܚ ܦܩܕ ܒܝ
ܡܫܡܫܝܢ ܕܢܗܘܐ ܫܡܫܐ ܘܕܬܬܦܚܘܢ ܐܘܪܚܐ. ܘܐܬܡܢܝܬ ܘܐܬܬܟܘ
ܘܐܬܦܢܝ ܘܕܗܘܦܟܗܘܢ ܠܘܬ ܫܡܫܐ ܐܝܟ ܕܥܒܕ ܕܒܝܫܬܐ ܠܐ ܙܟܐ.
ܘܐܬܟܢܫܘ ܕܒܬܪܐ ܥܡ ܘܬܘܒ ܐܬܦܢܝܘ ܠܗ ܐܦ ܩܐܬܘܠܝܩܐ ܕܦܬܓܡ̈ܝܐ
ܘܡܫܐܠܝܢ ܗ̇ܘܘ ܠܗ ܘܡܬܟܫܦܝܢ ܗ̇ܘܘ ܒܦܘܡܗ ܟܠ ܟܠܬܐ ܕܡܫܠܛܐ ܗ̇ܘ
ܡܢܗ ܡܢ ܬܚܝܬ ܫܘܠܛܢܐ ܒܐܪܥܐ ܕܐܬܚܣܢܐ. ܗ̇ܘ ܕܝܢ ܐܘܦ ܐܪܬܘܕܘܟܣܐ
ܘܟܠܗܘܢ ܒܢ̈ܝ ܬܪܥܝܬܗ ܡܫܡܫܢܬܐ ܒܢ̈ܘܟܪܝܘܬܗܘܢ ܐܠܗܐ ܐܝܟ ܠܗܘܢ ܠܥܠܡ
ܦܬܓܡܐ ܘܬܫܒܘܚܬܐ ܘܫܘܒܚܐ ܘܐܡܪܘ ܠܗܘܢ ܕܢܦܫ ܠܗ ܡܫܠܛ ܬܘܕܝܬܐ
ܐܡܝܢܝܢ ܡܣܪܘܬܐ ܟܠ ܦܬܓܡܐ ܕܐܬܚܣܢ ܘܐܦܢܝܢ ܠܝ ܩܐܬܘܠܝܩܐ ܐܠܐ
ܡܫܠܛ ܕܢܐܬܘܢ ܠܟܢܘܫܝܘܬܐ ܗܢܐ ܕܐܬܚܣܢܬ ܦܪ̈ܝ ܡܫܬܦܝ ܟܠ ܒܢ̈ܝ
ܢܫܬܘܬܦܘܢ ܕܒܟܠܗ ܡܢ ܚܕܐ ܟܠܗ ܡܐܪܟܝ ܕܠܐܬܚܣܢ. ܘܡܢ ܦܬܓܡܐ ܘܦܬܓܡ̈ܐ
ܘܬܘܒܥܘܬܐ ܘܫܡܫܐ ܕܐܝܬ ܒܫܢܝܐ ܐܬܪܘܬܐ ܟܠ ܗ̇ܢ ܐܦܢܝܢ ܠܝ ܦܪܝܫܐ

ܡܬܘܠܝܬܐ. ܘܗܘܐ ܐܬܝܢ ܒܫܝܢܐ ܘܒܢܝܚܐ. ܟܕ ܐܢܫ ܗܠܝܢ ܡ̈ܠܟܐ ܢܘܟܪ̈ܝܐ
ܐܬܬܛܝܒܘ ܗܠܝܢ ܒܥܬܕܐ ܘܠܡܫܬܡܥܢܘܬܐ ܘܩܪܒܘ ܢܦܫܗ ܠܗܘܢ ܫܡܫܐ ܐܝܟ
ܘܫܡܥܘ ܠܗܘܢ ܡܬܦܪܣܘܟܠܬܐ ܡܢ ܢܫܛܘܪܝܐ ܒܛܘܒܢܐ ܡܪܝ ܠܐ ܝܕܥܘ
ܗ̇ܘܘ ܢܠܗܘܢ ܘܙܐܦܐ ܕܠܘܩܒܠܗܘܢ ܡܫܡܠܝܬܐ. ܘܗܘܘ ܗܢܐ ܟܕܝܐ ܗܘ
ܡܬܝܕܥ ܠܘܬܗܘܢ ܕܡܟܐ ܠܛܘܪܟܝܐ. ܕܟܠ ܐܡܬܝ ܕܢܦܩ ܐܦܣܩܘܦܐ
ܕܠܗܘܢ ܐܠܝܢ ܠܘܬ ܢܫܛܘܪܝܐ ܘܢܦܩܝܢ ܠܗܘܢ ܐܚܪܢܐ ܚܠܦܘܗܝ ܡܢ
ܦܛܪܝܩܘܣ. ܘܐܬܐ ܒܡܕܝܢܬܐ ܚܕܬܐ ܗܢܐ ܕܝܬܒܐ ܕܐܡܪܝܢ ܡܢ ܟܠܟܠ.
ܘܗܘܘ ܦܐܪܐ ܠܗܘܢ ܒܥܢܝܐ ܘܡܬܡܟܟܢܐ. ܘܗܠܝܢ ܒܩܘܦܐ ܠܛܘܪܟܝܐ
ܕܡܫܬܚܠܦܢ ܒܥܒܪܐ ܐܦܠܝܢ ܘܠܚܡܐ ܦܐܝܢ ܘܠܐ ܫܡܥ ܐܝܬ ܠܗܘܢ ܦܘܪܩܢܐ
ܕܡܬܦܠܓܬܐ ܐܠܐ ܒܠܚܘܕ ܐܦܠܝܢ ܒܬܐܪܐ ܕܚܡܬܐ. ܘܟܕ ܐܡܪ ܗܠܝܢ ܒܢ̈ܝܐ
ܡܫܬܒܪܝܢ ܕܐܬܝܢ ܗܘܘ ܝܕܥܐ ܟܕ ܠܐ ܐܬܝܢ ܗܘܘ. ܘܝܕܥܝܢ ܗܘܘ ܒܠܗܘܢ ܕܒܬܐ
ܠܘܬܗܘܢ ܐܬܝܢ ܠܛܘܪܟܝܐ ܘܡܪܢܐ ܐܚܝ ܕܝܠܢ. ܘܐܦ ܫܡܫܐ ܐܝܟ ܡܢ
ܢܫܛܘܪܝܐ ܡܬܒܠܝܢ ܒܛܘܒܢܐ ܟܕ ܠܐ ܫܡܥ ܝܕܥܝܢ ܠܢܦܫܗܘܢ ܘܠܐܦܝܗܘܢ
ܘܪܘܫܗܘܢ. ܘܡܬܝܕܥܝܢ ܚܕ ܟܢܫܐ ܡܫܒܚܐ ܕܠܛܘܪܟܝܐ ܦܝܫܬܐ ܗܘ
ܡܠܟܬܐ ܕܐܠܗܐ ܡܬܝܕܥܝܢ ܕܐܬܐ ܠܢܦܫܐ ܘܡܬܩܪܒܐ ܘܐܘܣܦܐ ܘܡܩܒܠܢܘܗ
ܘܡܫܬܠܗ ܕܐܝܟ ܠܝ. ܗܕܐ ܐܬܝܢ ܠܘܬܗܘܢ ܦܪܝܫܐ. ܘܒܠܝܠܝܐ
ܕܡܫܬܒܚ ܠܘܬܗܘܢ ܕܝܠܗ ܒܦܪܘ ܐܚܪ ܕܢܝܚܐ ܒܡܕܝܢܬܐ ܦܬܟܝܢ ܠܗ.
ܘܡܬܗܘܢ ܒܥܠܗܘܢ ܡܬܩܒܠܝܢ ܠܟܠ ܒܪ ܕܐܬܠܝܢ. ܘܡܬܕܪܝܢ ܒܐܝܟܪܐ
ܪܒܐ ܡܬܩܒܠܝܢ ܠܗܘܢ ܘܕܘܒܪܐ ܕܡܕܝܢܬܐ ܘܕܫܘܪܪܐ ܫܦܝܪ ܪܚܡܝܢ ܡܬܪ
ܡܢ ܟܠ ܒܡܬܡܢ̈ܐ. ܘܫܦܪܐ ܐܚܪܢܐ ܫܦܪ ܡܢ ܗܢܐ ܕܝܠܝ ܠܐ ܝܕܥܝܢ ܘܠܐ
ܫܡܥ ܡܬܒܠܝܢ. ܘܒܗܢܐ ܫܦܪܐ ܕܝܠܝ ܫܘܪܝܐ ܒܬܒܝܢ ܘܩܪܝܢ ܒܬܩܐ
ܕܠܘܩܒܠܗܝܢ ܠܗܘܢ ܕܐܬܠܝܢ ܒܬܩܐ ܘܕܡܬܒܠܝܢ ܠܛܘܪܟܝܐ ܫܦܝܪܐ.
ܘܒܠܚܘܕܝܗܘܢ ܠܛܘܪܟܝܐ ܡܬܩܒܠܝܢ ܠܗܘܢ ܠܒܬܩܐ ܟܠ ܒܢܝܢܝܗܘܢ ܟܕ
ܠܚܡܐ ܫܦܝܪܐ ܕܡܢ ܢܦܫܗ ܡܫܝܚܐ ܐܠܗܐ ܘܠܚܡܐ ܕܡܬܝܗܒ ܡܢ ܐܠܗܐ
ܠܐ ܫܡܥ ܡܬܩܪܒܝܢ ܕܢܦܫܗܘܢ ܐܝܟ ܠܠܚܡܐ ܠܛܘܪܟܝܐ ܐܠܐ ܩܪܝܢ ܠܗܘܢ
ܗܘܝ ܒܠܚܡܐ ܕܝܠܝ ܫܦܘܪܐ. ܘܐܦ ܠܚܡܐ ܕܡܬܠܐ ܒܗ ܡܫܬܪܐ ܒܠܚܡܐ
ܠܛܘܪܟܝܐ ܠܘܬ ܡܬܩܒܠܝܢ ܠܗܘܢ ܐܝܟ ܕܡܫܬܒܚ ܒܠܗ ܒܢܦܫܗܘܢ ܡܠܐ
ܩܪܝܢ ܘܡܠܐ ܡܬܩܒܠܝܢ. ܒܫܘܒܚܬܐ ܕܝܢ ܕܝܘܡܐ ܩܕܝܫܐ ܕܐܪܒܥܝܢ ܠܐ

ܐܚܪ̈ܢܝܢ ܒܣܦܪܐ ܚܕܬܐ ܘܦܢ̈ܝܬܐ ܐܠܐ ܒܣܦܪܐ ܕܝܗܒ ܐܝܟ ܦܬ̈ܓܡܐ. ܘܡܢ ܗܪܟܐ
ܡܢ ܪܡܫܐ ܠܪܡܫܐ ܐܚܪ̈ܢܝܢ ܘܦܘܪ̈ܥܢܐ ܕܐܪ̈ܐ ܩܪ̈ܒܐ ܘܫܠܛ̈ܢܐ ܡܢ ܠܚܡܛܐ
ܕܟܝܢܐ ܕܫ̈ܢܝܐ ܡܫܬܟܠܝܢ ܠܗܘܢ ܒ ܒܬܫܡܫܬܐ ܪܒܬܐ ܘܒܫܘܒܚܬܐ
ܡܫܪ̈ܝܢ ܠܐܬ̈ܘܬܐ ܘܡܬܚܫܒܝܢ ܦܬܓܡܐ ܕܟܝܢܐ ܕܡܢ ܫܡ̈ܝܐ ܕܟܝ̈ܢܬܐ ܘܫܪܟܝܢ
ܡܘܪ̈ܟܢܐ ܘܗܘܒܠܐ ܐܦ ܐܩܦܬܐ ܡܫܬܚܠܦܝܢ ܡܢ ܐܬ̈ܘܬܐ ܩܫܝܫܐ ܘܡܫܢܝܢ
ܒܚܕ ܢܦܩܐ ܠܒܥܠܐ ܕܡܘܪܟܢܐ. ܘܐܫܬܡܠܝܘ ܗܢܘܢ ܐܬ̈ܘܬܐ ܕܐܬ̈ܘܬܐ
ܫ̈ܢܝܐ ܘܟܠܗ ܒܠܗ ܕܡܢܚܬܐ ܠܚܫܐ ܐܚܪܝܐ ܕܡܬܚܫܒܐ ܢܒܗܘܢ ܘܫܦܝܪܐ
ܕܠܗܘܢ ܒܠܚܘܕܝܗܘܢ. ܘܡܢ ܬܡܢ ܘܠܗܠ ܐܝܬ ܬܘܒ ܡܢ̈ܝܢܬܐ ܫܦܝܪ̈ܬܐ
ܘܐܝܬ ܒܗܝܢ ܒܡܠܐ ܬܘܪܒܐ ܚܙ̈ܝܐ ܫܦܝܪ̈ܝܢ ܠܟܠܒ̈ܬܐ ܕܐܝܬ ܠܗܘܢ ܫܦܝܪܐ
ܒܠܚܘܕܝܗܘܢ ܘܗܘܝܢ ܡܬܚܫܒܝܢ ܕܬܪܝܢ ܡܪ̈ܚܐ ܐܚܪ̈ܢܐ. ܘܡܢܝܢܬܐ ܒܪܝܬܐ ܡܬܚܫܒܐ
ܦܪܘܫ[ܡܠ] ܘܫܡܟܐ ܕܡܬܟܒܢ ܐܝܟܢܐ. ܘܡܢ ܬܡܢ ܒܬܪ ܐܝܟ ܡܬܕܡܝܐ
ܕܡܫܡܐ ܡܘܡܬܐ ܘܟܠܟ ܠܐܪܥܐ ܗܢ ܕܡܫܬܢܝܢ ܒܗ ܬܘܪܒܐ ܕܐܬܝܗܘܢ
ܒܪܫܝܬܐ ܐܝܟ ܕܐܡܪܝܢ ܡܢ ܠܒܠܒ. ܘܐܬܝܗܘܢ ܐܝܟܐ ܡܬܡܫܡܫܢܐ ܦܪ̈ܝܫܐ
ܘܒܠܒ [ܐܠܗܐ]. ܘܐܬܝܗܘܢ ܒܡܫܬܪ ܒܦܫܡܬܐ ܕܠܐ ܡܬܚܫܒܐ ܘܠܐ ܡܘܬܐ
ܘܠܐ ܒܬ̈ܐ ܐܠܐ ܐܬܝܗܘܢ ܒܬܪܒܐ ܘܐܬܝܗܘܢ ܡܬܚܫܒܐ ܘܪܘܒܬܐ ܘܡܬܚܫܒܬܐ
ܘܡܫܬܟܠܝܢ ܡܢ ܕܘܒܬܐ ܠܘܒܬܐ ܘܐܝܬ ܠܗܘܢ ܡܢܝܢܐ ܫܦܝܪ̈ܐ ܒܬܐ ܘܬܘܪܐ
ܘܦܬܓܡܐ ܘܫܘܫܡܐ ܘܐܝܬ ܠܒܠܚܘܕ ܡܢ ܦܬܓܡܐ ܗܠܝܢ ܬܪܝܢ ܒܘܪܒܠܝܬܐ
ܐܝܟ ܫܠܡܐ. ܘܐܬܝܗܘܢ ܐܪܒܥܐ ܡܠܟ̈ܐ ܪܘܪ̈ܒܐ ܘܡܫܬܡܫܢܐ ܚܕ ܠܘܬ ܡܢ ܚܕ.
ܘܡܫܬܡܫܢܘܢ ܕܡܠܟ̈ܐ ܗܠܝܢ ܐܬܝܗܘܢ ܦܘܪ̈ܫܢ ܘܬܪܝܢ ܦܘܪ̈ܫܢ ܘܕܬܠܬܐ
ܫܡܗܘܢ ܘܕܐܪܒܥܐ ܠܘܬܗ ܘܫܡܐ ܦܘܪܫܢܐ ܠܒܠܚܘܕܝܗܘܢ ܬܬܪ. ܘܫܡܐ ܐܪܒܥܗܘܢ
ܦܪܝܫܝܢ. ܘܡܬܐܡܪܐ ܕܠܒܠܚܘܕ ܡܢ ܗܠܝܢ ܡܠܟ̈ܐ ܐܝܟ ܒܫܡܗ ܐܪܒܥܡܐܐ
ܠܠܫ̈ܢܐ ܒܠܫ̈ܢܐ ܒܡܫܬܪܝܬܐ. ܘܪܘܚ ܐܪܒܥܗܘܢ ܒܪܫܐ ܠܫܡܝܐ ܡܬܚܫܒܬܐ
ܕܫܡ̈ܝܐ. ܘܠܗ ܡܢܗܘܢ ܒܠܗܘܢ ܫ̈ܢܝܐ ܐܬܝܗܘܢ. ܗܠܝܢ ܕܝܢ ܬܘܪܒܐ
ܒܪܫܡܫܬܐ ܕܐܡܪܝܢ ܢܦܫܝܢ ܫܡܫܐ ܐܝܟ ܕܒܗܘܢܬܐ ܡܢ ܐܦܫܘܫܬܐ
ܕܥܠܗ ܒܝܗ ܡܬܚܫܒܐ ܪܒܬܐ ܗܢ ܕܫ̈ܢܝܐ ܕܐܬܝܗܘܢ ܫܡܫ ܒܬܪ̈ܬܐ
ܪܒܬܐ. ܘܗܠܝܢ ܬܘܪܒܐ ܒܪܫܡܫܬܐ ܒܡܫܬܪ ܒܦܫܡܬܐ ܘܒܪܝܬܐ ܐܝܬ
ܠܗܘܢ ܡܢܗܘܢ ܒܫܢܝܐ ܘܡܫܬܡܫܢܐ ܘܕܝܢܐ. ܘܬܪܬܝܢ ܒܪܝܬܐ ܐܝܬ ܠܗܘܢ
ܒܡܠܗܘܢ ܫܡܝܐ. ܘܢܦܫܝܢ ܢܦܘܩܐ ܘܡܬܪܝܢ ܒܗܠܝܢ ܒܠܫܢܐ ܕܠܐ ܫܘܪܝܐ.

ܘܡܫܬܡܠܝܢ ܐܬܪ̈ܐ ܒܠܗܘܢ ܕܡܕܒܪܢܘܬܐ ܦܪܘܫܘܬܐ ܕܡܢ ܢܦܫܗ ܡܫܝܚܐ
ܒܟܠ ܐܬܪ̈ܐ ܒܫܘܡܠܝܗ ܐܒܘܗ̈ܝ ܘܠܐܪ̈ܥܢ ܐܝܟ ܚܕ̈ܢܐ ܐܠܐ ܒܡܕܝܢ ܒܡܟܬܒܢܘܬܐ
ܘܒܡܟܬܒܢܘܬܗܘܢ ܩܕܝܫܐ ܐܒܘܗ̈ܝ. ܘܡܘܕܝܢ ܡܫܝܚܐ ܡܟܝܬ ܐܠܗܐ ܘܐܡܪܝܢ ܡܫܝܚܐ
ܐܠܗܐ ܘܢܗܝܢ ܠܟܬܒܐ ܘܠܡܫܒܚܘܬܐ ܐܝܟ ܕܒܫܘܬܦܘܬܐ ܒܠܗܘܢ. ܘܠܡܫܝܚܐ
ܗܘ ܠܗܘܢ ܒܐܪ̈ܥܬܗܘܢ ܘܠܐ ܙܟܝܐ ܘܠܐ ܒܪܢܫܐ ܘܠܐ ܡܫܝܚܐ ܘܠܐ ܐܦܩܬܐ ܐܠܐ
ܒܠܗ ܡܬܒܠܬܗܘܢ ܒܦܓܪܐ ܘܡܠܟܐ ܕܟܠܐ ܐܠܗܘܬܗ ܘܢܦܫܐ ܗܘܝܐ ܐܝܬ
ܠܗܘܢ. ܘܝܠܦ ܠܗ ܗܕܐ ܒܟܠܬܐ ܒܒܝܬܐ ܗܘ ܕܒܗ ܐܬܬܚܝܪ ܢܣܛܘܪܐ ܒܟܠ
ܒܫܘܬܦܘܬܐ ܕܒܐܪ̈ܥܬܐ ܕܒܫܘܬܦܐ ܒܐܝܕ̈ܝ ܗܘ ܠܗܠܝܢ ܒܢܝ̈ ܐܢܫܐ ܕܒܪܘܚܐ ܗܘ
ܕܫܡܥ ܩܕܡ ܐܠܗ̈ܐ ܒܗܘܢ ܘܕܝܢ̈ܐ ܘܡܫܝܚ̈ܐ ܘܒܢܝܐ ܡܬܩܪܝܢܐ ܘܫܘܝܐ
ܙܒܢܐ ܕܠܐ ܡܬܝܕܥܐ ܘܡܘܫܚܬܐ. ܘܡܢ ܗܕܐ ܒܟܠܬܐ ܙܪܥ ܢܘܪܐ ܦܪܝܫܐ ܘܠܐ
ܢܣܒ ܕܢܦܩ ܠܐܬܪܐ. ܡܛܠ ܐܬܝܕܥ ܕܐܦ ܢܘܪܐ ܕܐܠܗܐ ܠܐ ܦܪܐ ܘܢܣܒ ܒܟܠ
ܐܬܪܐ ܕܡܬܩܪܝܢ ܗܢܘܢ ܐܬܬܣܝܡܬ ܡܛܠ ܢܘܪܐ ܕܫܘܝܐ ܢܣܒܬܐ ܒܟܠ ܡܢ
ܒܢܝ̈ܗܘܢ ܘܒܟܠ ܦܘܪ̈ܫܢܝܗܘܢ. ܘܐܟܚܕܐ ܕܗܢܘܢ ܕܡܬܚܙܐ ܗܘ̇ ܡܢ ܦܘܪܐ
ܦܪܨܘܦܐ ܦܪܝܫ ܡܬܦܬܟܪܢܘܬܗ ܒܝܬ ܦܪܣܐ ܕܡܬܚܙܐ ܗܘܐ ܦܘܡܗ ܗܢܘܢ
ܕܡܬܚܙܐ ܡܢܗ ܡܟܬܒܢܘܬܐ ܕܦܪܣܐ ܒܟܠܗ. ܘܗܘܝܐ ܐܝܠܝܢ ܕܦܘܬܚܬܐ
ܢܦܩܬܐ ܕܡܠܦܢܘܬܐ ܦܪܝܫ ܦܪܨܘܦ ܘܐܡܪܝܢ ܢܣܒ ܗܘܐ ܢܘܪܐ ܦܪܝܫܐ
ܒܠܗܘܢ ܘܟܠ ܦܘܪ̈ܫܢܝܗܘܢ ܘܟܠ ܡܬܒܢܝܗܘܢ ܒܬܪ ܕܝܢ ܦܪܨܘܦ
ܘܦܪܨܘܦ ܠܡܫܡܥܬܐ ܦܪܝܫܬܐ ܘܢܦܫܗ ܠܗܘܢ ܡܢ ܛܘܪܐ ܕܚܢ̈ܐ ܐܬܬܚܪܝܡܘ
ܘܐܫܬܠܡܘ ܠܐ ܦܫ ܠܗܘܢ ܢܘܪܐ ܦܪܝܫܐ ܐܠܐ ܢܘܪܐ ܕܝܗܝܒܘܬܐ ܘܕܫܘܬܦܐ.
ܘܗܘܘ ܦܫܝܩܐ ܘܡܫܬܠܡܐ ܡܢ ܡܟܬܒܢܘܬܐ ܘܡܢ ܒܝܬܘܬܐ ܘܡܢ ܒܠܗܘܢ
ܐܬܪܐ ܕܝܪܬܐ ܦܪܝܫܬܐ. ܡܛܠ ܐܠܗܐ ܢܦܘܩ ܠܝ ܡܢ ܚܘܠܫܐ ܘܦܘܬܦܘܬܐ
ܕܡܬܚܙܝܢ ܐܦ ܠܒܠܗܘܢ ܡܛܠܗ ܕܝܪܬܐ ܦܪܝܫܬܐ ܒܝܬ ܙܒܢ̈ܐ ܕܡܛܠ
ܐܠܗܐ ܡܛܠ ܘܕܒܠܗܘܢ ܦܪ̈ܝܫܐ. ܘܠܐܠܗܐ ܦܘܚܡܐ ܘܟܠ ܒܠܝ ܫܘܒܚܗ
ܘܝܩܪܗ ܠܥܠܡ ܥܠܡܝܢ ܐܡܝܢ.

ܫܠܡܬ ܐܓܪܬܐ ܕܩܕܝܫܐ ܡܪܝ ܦܝܠܘܟܣܝܢܘܣ ܐܦܝܣܩܘܦܐ ܕܡܒܘܓ
ܕܠܘܬ ܐܒܘܥܦܪ ܐܣܛܪܛܠܛܘܣ ܕܚܝܪܬܐ ܕܢܥܡܢ.

www.ingramcontent.com/pod-product-compliance
Ingram Content Group UK Ltd.
Pitfield, Milton Keynes, MK11 3LW, UK
UKHW021306180426
11947UKWH00015B/1059